Holly Hassel · Christie Launius · Susan Rensing

A Guide to Teaching Introductory Women's and Gender Studies

Socially Engaged Classrooms

AF173396

palgrave
macmillan

Holly Hassel
North Dakota State University
Fargo, ND, USA

Christie Launius
Kansas State University
Manhattan, KS, USA

Susan Rensing
Kansas State University
Manhattan, KS, USA

ISBN 978-3-030-71784-1   ISBN 978-3-030-71785-8   (eBook)
https://doi.org/10.1007/978-3-030-71785-8

© The Editor(s) (if applicable) and The Author(s) 2021
This work is subject to copyright. All rights are solely and exclusively licensed by the Publisher, whether the whole or part of the material is concerned, specifically the rights of translation, reprinting, reuse of illustrations, recitation, broadcasting, reproduction on microfilms or in any other physical way, and transmission or information storage and retrieval, electronic adaptation, computer software, or by similar or dissimilar methodology now known or hereafter developed.
The use of general descriptive names, registered names, trademarks, service marks, etc. in this publication does not imply, even in the absence of a specific statement, that such names are exempt from the relevant protective laws and regulations and therefore free for general use.
The publisher, the authors and the editors are safe to assume that the advice and information in this book are believed to be true and accurate at the date of publication. Neither the publisher nor the authors or the editors give a warranty, expressed or implied, with respect to the material contained herein or for any errors or omissions that may have been made. The publisher remains neutral with regard to jurisdictional claims in published maps and institutional affiliations.

Cover design by eStudioCalamar

This Palgrave Macmillan imprint is published by the registered company Springer Nature Switzerland AG
The registered company address is: Gewerbestrasse 11, 6330 Cham, Switzerland

A Guide to Teaching Introductory Women's and Gender Studies

"In *A Guide to Teaching Introductory Women's and Gender Studies: Socially Engaged Classrooms*, Hassel, Launius, and Rensing have written a tiny tour-de-force that walks the talk of Women's and Gender Studies. The authors succinctly explore not only *what* but also *how* and *why* students learn in a well-designed intro WGS course. I can think of no other text that so effectively prepares instructors teaching Women's and Gender Studies for the first time, or the thirty-first time."

—Nancy Chick, *Director of the Endeavor Foundation Center for Faculty Development and Professor of English, Rollins College, USA*

"Hassel, Launius, and Rensing have written a vital text for those who teach a vital class: the introductory course in women's and gender studies. This book is a much-needed jolt of energy and reminder of the possibilities that WGS offers for our students. Based on extensive research and an impressive range of practical experience, *A Guide to Teaching Introductory Women's and Gender Studies* will be the go-to resource for teachers in the field."

—Kevin Gannon, *Director of the Center for Excellence in Teaching and Learning and Professor of History, Grand View University, USA*

"In *A Guide to Teaching Introductory Women's and Gender Studies*, Hassel, Launius, and Rensing reflect on their classroom practice, share evidence-based approaches, and pose critical questions to help readers clarify their curricular goals for this crucial course that serves as a gateway to the WGS degree. This book is an invaluable resource for new instructors and experienced professors alike."

—Jennifer Musial, *Assistant Professor of Women's and Gender Studies, New Jersey City University, USA*

"Rather than romanticize the labor of teaching the introductory course, Hassel, Launius, and Rensing take a sober – and yet hopeful – look at the potentials and challenges of feminist pedagogies in times of national and global crises. The thoughtful advice they provide reads as an invitation to new and seasoned feminist teachers to both rethink and reimagine our own commitments to engaged feminist pedagogies and curricular transformations."

—Dana M. Olwan, *Assistant Professor of Women's and Gender Studies, Syracuse University, USA*

Acknowledgments

So much has made this book possible. We are grateful to the University of Wisconsin's Women's and Gender Studies Consortium which brought the three of us together and became an incubator for the ideas and insights that we draw on for this guide. A special thanks goes to former Director Helen Klebesadel for all of her encouragement and support over the years.

Holly is thankful for the research funding she received from the University of Wisconsin Colleges (UWC) (now dissolved) in 2017–2018 that supported the scholarship of teaching and learning project that forms the foundation of this book. She also is thankful for the amazing colleagues she worked with in the UWC Gender, Sexuality, and Women's Studies program, where she had 15 years' worth of conversations about teaching, learning, and assessment that have influenced the shape of this book.

Christie would like to thank the Faculty Development program at the University of Wisconsin Oshkosh for granting her a sabbatical leave in the fall of 2017. The sabbatical leave was officially granted for work on a different project, but as is sometimes the case, ideas for new projects occur before ongoing ones are finished. Christie is eternally grateful to Holly and Susan for their willingness to be pitched on the idea for this book, and more importantly, for scrambling with her not only to write a prospectus for it, but also to imagine a SoTL project and obtain IRB approval, all in the space of a few months. Discussing student learning and writing this book with them has been a joy.

Susan would like to thank several colleagues past and present whose thoughtful conversation about student learning in the Intro course has shaped her ideas in this book: Erin Winterrowd, Geneva Murray, Alicia Johnson, and Rachel Levitt. She would also like to thank all of her students who make teaching the Intro course so meaningful. And special thanks go to Christie and Susan's son, Porter, who brought good humor as his parents worked hard to find time to write this book during his preschool years.

About This Book

This book provides a practical, evidence-based guide to teaching introductory Women's and Gender Studies (WGS) courses. Based on the findings of a Scholarship of Teaching and Learning project that analyzed the written work of 72 Intro to WGS students, the authors equip instructors with key principles for approaching the class that can help them adapt their pedagogy to a range of classroom environments. By putting student learning at the center of course design, the authors invite readers to reflect on their own investments in and goals for the introductory courses they teach. The book also draws on the authors' combined decades of experience teaching the introductory course at a variety of institutions, and aims to help instructors anticipate the emotional, intellectual, and interpersonal challenges and rewards of teaching and learning in the introductory WGS course. Chapters focus on course design, including identifying desired learning outcomes (in terms of course content, skills, *and* dispositions or habits of mind); choosing course materials; pedagogical activities; and assessing student learning.

This book will be an invaluable resource for experienced WGS instructors and those seeking or planning to teach it for the first time, including graduate students and high school teachers.

Contents

About the Authors

Holly Hassel is Professor of English at North Dakota State University in Fargo, ND. Previously, she taught writing and women's and gender studies at the University of Wisconsin-Marathon County, a two-year college, for 16 years. She is the co-author, with Christie Launius, of *Threshold Concepts in Women's and Gender Studies*, 2nd ed. (Routledge, 2018) and co-edited the 2017 collection, *Surviving Sexism in Academia: Feminist Strategies for Leadership*, with Kirsti Cole.

Christie Launius is Associate Professor and Head of the Gender, Women, and Sexuality Studies Department at Kansas State University. With Holly Hassel, she is co-author of the introductory textbook *Threshold Concepts in Women's and Gender Studies*. She co-edited the *Routledge International Handbook of Working-Class Studies* (2021) and serves as Book Review Editor for the *Journal of Working-Class Studies*.

Susan Rensing is Teaching Associate Professor of Gender, Women, and Sexuality Studies at Kansas State University. She has taught multiple sections of the introductory WGS course every semester for the last 13 years and has been recognized for her distinguished teaching. In addition to her research interests in student learning and inclusive pedagogy, she also specializes in health equity and reproductive justice.

List of Figures

List of Tables

1

Introduction

Why write a book about teaching the introductory women's and gender studies course, or more broadly, courses that introduce students to socially engaged academic disciplines? Because, we contend, when done well, such an introductory course has the capacity to transform students' lives and cultivate their capacity for lifelong civic engagement, whether it serves as a gateway to pursuing an undergraduate major or minor in the field, or as the one and only WGS course a student ever takes.

This view and understanding of the course may stand in contrast to some instructors' belief that the course is an "easy prep" because of its introductory nature, or a staple part of one's teaching load that becomes a bit rote and boring over time because it is at a basic level. Still others see teaching the introductory course as a dreaded task because many students who take it do so not out of a desire to engage the material but merely to fulfill a requirement; as such, the notion is that the introductory course is where we are most likely to encounter the resistance of students who have internalized anti-feminist beliefs and attitudes or simply are not engaged with or invested in the topic and questions of the course. While not discounting the grains of truth in the characterizations above, we instead see the introductory course as being deeply challenging but also rewarding and *vital* work.

On a practical level, we believe that a book on the introductory WGS course is warranted for a number of reasons. First and foremost, this attention recognizes the role that introductory courses play in introducing students to the field, and potentially recruiting them to undergraduate major and minor

© The Author(s), under exclusive license to Springer Nature
Switzerland AG 2021
H. Hassel et al., *A Guide to Teaching Introductory Women's and Gender Studies*,
https://doi.org/10.1007/978-3-030-71785-8_1

programs. Only rarely do students arrive at college intending to declare a major or minor in WGS; indeed, women's and gender studies courses are still relatively rare at the secondary level, though there have been gains and progress in recent years.[1] As we note below, more students arrive on campus with knowledge of feminism and feminist and other social justice movements than in the past, but that doesn't necessarily translate into an awareness of the academic field of women's and gender studies. Instead, a typical pathway to the major or minor is through the introductory course, increasingly taken in order to fulfill a general-education requirement. Of course, Women's and Gender Studies is not the only field that has relatively little presence at the secondary level; these programs thus rely heavily on attracting students to their majors through their general-education offerings. For Women's and Gender Studies, reaching students in their first and second year on campus is a perennial challenge. Given this, we agree with Hobbs and Rice's assertion that

> Introductory undergraduate courses, intentionally or not, "brand" the field, and with it the department or program. They construct a program's identity while giving students a taste of the broader fare available for consumption at the upper years. *Student reaction to the 'gateway' course can either make or break the viability of the undergraduate degree program.* (pp. 139–140 emphasis added)

Whether approaching the issue idealistically or pragmatically, careful attention to planning and teaching the introductory course seems wise.

If a book about teaching the introductory course is warranted because of the crucial role it plays in introducing students to the field and potentially attracting them to take further coursework, the question of who is teaching the course, and how, immediately follows. There is an increasing number of people earning Ph.D.s in the field. As White and Musial note, "Between 2008 and 2016, the number of Gender, Women's, and Feminist Studies (GWFS) Ph.D. programs nearly doubled" (p. 4); they report 23 programs in the United States and Canada as of 2016. Given this development, a growing number of doctoral students are receiving training and mentorship in teaching in the field, whether in the form of a proseminar, or possibly a course on feminist pedagogies. Indiana University, for example, has a course called Gender Studies Pedagogy and Theory, Rutgers University offers a similar course called Feminist Pedagogies, and SUNY Albany offers

---

[1]For example, the 2017 NWSA conference included a one day teach-in for K-12 teachers and librarians, organized by Ileana Jimenez, Stephanie Troutman, and Karsonya Wise Whitehead. Jimenez also created the hashtags #HSfeminism and #K12feminism and has maintained a blog, Feminist Teacher, since 2009. See Kessler (2018), Merlin (2017), Hill (2013), and Kim and Ringrose (2018).

Advanced Feminist Pedagogy and Theory to graduate students who teach their undergraduate Introduction to Feminisms course. At the University of Pennsylvania, students pursuing the graduate certificate in Gender, Sexuality, and Women's Studies may fulfill part of their requirements through attending the program's Pedagogy Seminars, and may create and submit a syllabus for a GSWS course.

An increasing number of people are earning graduate degrees in the field, are gaining knowledge about and experience with feminist pedagogies while in graduate school, and are designing introductory courses from that place of knowledge and training. Nonetheless, it continues to be the reality that many who teach the course did not prepare to do so as graduate students. This is perhaps especially true for academics who teach at smaller institutions, both private and public, where Women's and Gender Studies programs are less likely to be freestanding departments with their own tenure lines. WGS courses in these institutions are often staffed by people with disciplinary degrees on loan from their "home" departments, though many have some graduate-level coursework in Women's and Gender Studies. In other words, many people find themselves teaching the introductory course who were not explicitly hired to do so. As Musial and White note, there is a "fraught politics around whom–and with what training–is considered qualified to teach it" (p. 4). We are certainly sympathetic to the position of those who have earned a Ph.D. in Women's and Gender Studies and who decry the fact that many who teach the introductory course are not credentialed to do so. But as academics who taught for many years at underfunded public two-year campuses and four-year regional comprehensives, we are also fully aware that in many cases, if it were not for the willingness of faculty with disciplinary degrees to teach WGS courses, there would be none taught.

When preparing to teach the introductory course for the first time, whether one is a graduate student in WGS or a faculty member coming to the course from a primarily disciplinary background, there is a learning curve that requires assessing one's own areas of expertise and pedagogical values. Our hope in this book is to reach both of the aforementioned audiences and address what we believe is a real need in higher education, and in the field of women's and gender studies more specifically. A third audience we have in mind are experienced instructors of the introductory course who are looking to revisit, reflect on, refresh, and revise their syllabi and their teaching. And finally, we imagine, too, that—as the title suggests—instructors from a range of other fields that are interdisciplinary and engaged in civic and social learning outside the classroom walls will find this text helpful, particularly courses in those fields that focus on social justice, diversity, inclusion, and equity. In the chapters that follow, readers will find a discussion of feminist pedagogical principles, insights we have gleaned about student learning in the introductory course, as well as concrete tools, tips, and strategies for designing and teaching it.

1.1   Approaching the Course

As the above discussion suggests, the Intro course can take many different forms and perform different functions in a given institutional context, with aims that at times can feel difficult to juggle. The Intro course on many campuses simultaneously serves as the gateway course for the WGS major and minor as well as a stand-alone course for general-education credit of a variety of types (fulfilling a requirement to take an interdisciplinary course, a social sciences or humanities course, or diversity or multicultural course). This reality presents Intro instructors with many tricky decisions, and often requires a balancing act both when it comes to choosing course material that is pitched at the appropriate level, and in cultivating one's teacherly persona.

But in addition to performing multiple simultaneous functions at the administrative level, instructors also bring different agendas and have different visions or approaches to teaching the Intro course. For example, some instructors feel strongly that the Intro course should provide a historical overview of feminist thought, others feel strongly that the course should introduce students to key theories and theorists, while others take a more topical approach. The three co-authors of *A Guide to Teaching Introductory to Women's and Gender Studies* have moved away from a coverage model and instead organize our courses around what we consider to be threshold concepts in the field, introducing students to the ways of seeing, thinking, and knowing that are valued by its practitioners. Put differently, we have adopted what Lendol Calder and other historians call a model of "uncoverage." We will return to this issue in more depth in Chapter 3, which focuses on choosing course materials and designing pedagogical activities that support student learning.

1.2   Where We're Coming from

As co-authors, we have been working together on projects for over a decade. Holly and Christie first met and began collaborating when they served as chairs of their respective Women's and Gender Studies (WGS) programs at institutions in the University of Wisconsin System (Christie at UW Oshkosh and Holly at a multi-campus, statewide, two-year college institution, the UW Colleges). As members of the University of Wisconsin System's Women's Studies Consortium (a group that met regularly to discuss shared interests of curriculum, campus climate, teaching, and outreach efforts), they recognized their shared interest in access and inclusion in higher education as well as their shared interest in pedagogy, particularly in the introductory course. It was through this relationship (a group that Susan also participated in because of her role as a faculty member at UW Oshkosh) that the conversations about foundational knowledge in the field began, in part because of the transfer mission of the UW Colleges and the interest Holly had in aligning the curriculum, instruction, and preparation of students moving from the two-year campuses to the four-year campuses to do additional, more advanced coursework in Women's and Gender Studies.

This book project originated in 2017, as Holly and Christie were copy-editing the second edition of their co-authored textbook, *Threshold Concepts in Women's and Gender Studies: Ways of Seeing, Thinking, and Knowing*. They have also undertaken a Scholarship of Teaching and Learning (SoTL) project, the results of which were published in 2017 in the journal *Teaching and Learning Inquiry*. As a longtime colleague of Christie's, Susan's input into and feedback on the textbook and the SoTL project have been crucial; with this project, she formally joins us.

1.3 Context and Theoretical Frame

Our recommendations in this text are drawn from four main sources; first, as we noted above, each of us has taught the introductory course in WGS for many years. Between us, we have taught in a range of formats, at multiple institutions, and across a broad span of our careers, as graduate teaching assistants, while in non-tenure-track positions, and as Assistant, Associate, and Full Professors, primarily in the midwestern, mid-Atlantic, and southern United States. These include two-year colleges, regional comprehensives, and research-intensive universities in both urban and more rural locations, in face-to-face, online, and hybrid formats, and in time frames ranging from three-week to 16-week sessions. As such, we draw on our collective years of experience throughout.

Second, like most feminist educators, our approach to this book is deeply informed by feminist pedagogy and the scholarly tradition and conversations that have evolved over the last fifty years around creating learning spaces that are inclusive, interactive, and learner-centered. Informing our thinking is Carolyn Shrewsbury's classic article, "What Is Feminist Pedagogy?" in which she first spelled out "a vision of what education might be like but frequently is not" (p. 8). As Shrewsbury argued in 1993:

> This is a vision of the classroom as a liberatory environment in which we, teacher-student and student-teacher, act as subjects, not objects. Feminist pedagogy is engaged teaching/learning–engaged with self in a continuing reflective process; engaged actively with the material being studied; engaged with others in a struggle to get beyond our sexism and racism and classism and homophobia and other destructive hatreds and to work together to enhance our knowledge; engaged with the community, with traditional organizations, and with movements for social change. (p. 8)

Interest in feminist pedagogy is arguably as old as the field of women's and gender studies. There have been numerous anthologies and monographs written about feminist pedagogy, as well as countless articles, including those published in the journal *Feminist Teacher*, which was founded in 1984. More specifically, we have found much inspiration and food for thought in the subset of books and articles devoted to the introductory course in particular. DiPalma and Winkler's *Teaching Introduction to Women's Studies: Expectations and Strategies*, published in 1999, continues to be relevant; more recently, *Atlantis: Critical Studies in Gender, Culture, and Social Justice* devoted a special issue to the subject of teaching the introductory course in 2016. Many of the ideas from the scholarship on teaching the introductory course resonate with our approach and echo the ethos we strive to cultivate when teaching it.

One area that many writings about teaching the introductory course have explored is the idea of tailoring the course based on knowledge about the students at the institution at which you're teaching, as well as the culture and politics of the region. Writing about the introductory course, Catherine Orr discusses curriculum as narrative and asks "what story are we telling?" She writes, "My approach seeks to create the space to ask: Which audiences am I trying to teach? Which stories is that desired audience more likely to see themselves within? Which histories, movements, and identities do my students need to hear, and what is the relationship between those stories and the ones I feel obligated to tell?" (pp. 12–13). She suggests that considerations of "the local" can and perhaps should be taken into account when designing the Intro course. Our reflections on our teaching led us to the same conclusion; in fact, we see this as a key element in our pedagogy.

In the same issue of *Atlantis*, AnaLouise Keating reflects on what she terms "pedagogies of invitation,"[2] which she sees as a type of post-oppositional pedagogy. Pedagogies of invitation stand in contrast to oppositional pedagogy, which pits instructors against students. She writes, "Employing invitational pedagogies, I do not judge, condemn, or mock students' perspectives (regardless of how shocking/appalling these perspectives might seem). Nor do I impose my views *on* them. Instead, I remain open to students' views, while establishing a framework for the course that requires them to analyze their views in dialogue with the required readings. By so doing, I model an attitude of respectful open-mindedness and encourage students to adopt a similar approach" (p. 18). There are many reasons why we believe that pedagogies of invitation are so important. In our experience, sometimes the same students who give voice to victim-blaming ideology turn out themselves to be survivors; their victim blaming is an internalization of oppression. In this instance, a pedagogy of invitation opens up space and gives students time to do the emotional reckoning that is often necessary to come to terms with the implications of the course material for their own lives and subsequently to facilitate learning. Similarly, we have also had students who initially espouse bootstraps ideology or racial respectability politics, who themselves are members of marginalized groups. On the flip side are students who are members of dominant groups whose first response to material may be white fragility or whataboutism, but who are capable of pushing through that initial layer of resistance over time. Having seen first-hand many students working through their process in the situations sketched out above, we are also inspired by Catherine Denial's writing on a "pedagogy of kindness" and agree with Kevin Gannon's assessment that "To teach, and to care about doing it well enough and in a way that's just, equitable, and humane for our students and our communities, is a radical stance" (p. 50).

To clarify, pedagogies of invitation and kindness should not be confused with inviting students to debate a group's humanity, which is a bright red line that should not be crossed; instead, we see these pedagogies as cultivating students' metacognition and modeling for them why they might have blockages, defensiveness, and complicated responses to and feelings about the course material. A pedagogy of invitation is also about inviting students to reflect on and to be aware of what they're feeling, and what the voices in their heads are.

Third, we have been influenced by the scholarship on threshold concepts. The term was coined by Ray Land and Jan Meyer in the mid-aughts and, in

---

[2]A concept developed more fully in *Transformation Now!: Toward a Post-Oppositional Politics of Change* (Keating 2013).

the context of teaching and learning, refers to academic concepts that "can be considered as akin to a portal, opening up a new and previously inaccessible way of thinking" (p. xv). When a student has crossed the threshold of understanding, they have "a transformed way of understanding, or interpreting, or viewing something" (p. xv). The threshold concepts framework has been developed to help instructors focus on and better understand student learning, as well as to aid in curriculum development. We believe that it is a particularly useful model when focusing on learning in introductory courses, as the notion is that students cannot advance within a field of study until they have crossed the threshold of understanding with regard to particular field-specific concepts.

Since Meyer and Land began to develop the framework, practitioners in diverse fields have undertaken the task of identifying what they consider to be the threshold concepts of their discipline (or interdiscipline, as the case may be).[3] The threshold concepts model has been particularly generative for the three of us, inspiring us to ask and try to answer a number of questions about our teaching and our students' learning; not only what do we want students to know and to know how to do as a result of taking the introductory course, but also what does that learning *look like*, how do we know whether it has taken place, and what factors facilitate and/or hinder that learning? Holly and Christie, with Susan's help, identified four threshold concepts in women's and gender studies and wrote a textbook, *Threshold Concepts in Women's and Gender Studies; Ways of Seeing, Thinking, and Knowing*, centered around them. We believe that organizing our introductory courses around the threshold concepts model makes transparent what we want students to learn and helps facilitate metacognitive conversations about what they are learning, and what skills they're acquiring. It also shines a light on what we as instructors consider to be the fundamental, most important, concepts and skills for students.

As the model has developed over the last two decades, researchers have articulated the characteristics of threshold concepts in any given field: they are transformative ("occasioning a significant shift in the perception of a subject"); integrative ("exposing the previously hidden interrelatedness of something"); irreversible ("unlikely to be forgotten, or unlearned only through considerable effort"); and the process of crossing the threshold

---

[3] See, for example, Winkler's "Racism as a Threshold Concept: Examining Learning in a 'Diversity Requirement' Course" (2017); Adsit's *Toward an Inclusive Creative Writing: Threshold Concepts to Guide the Literary Writing Curriculum* (2017); Adler-Kassner and Wardle's *Naming What We Know: Threshold Concepts of Writing Studies* (2015); and Townsend and Hanick's *Transforming Information Literacy Instruction: Threshold Concepts in Theory and Practice* (2016).

may entail an extended period of liminality,[4] ("a suspended state of partial understanding, or 'stuck place'"). Likewise, our own research emphasizes the discursive nature of threshold concepts. As will be seen below, the discursive nature of threshold concepts, as well as the concept of liminality in relation to student learning, were both key aspects of the research project we undertook to examine student learning in the introductory WGS course. The idea that many threshold concepts constitute troublesome knowledge also certainly rings true to those with experience teaching women's and gender studies.

Finally, and relatedly, our recommendations in this text are informed by insights gleaned from a classroom research project over the 2017–2018 academic year, across four sections of WAGS 201: Introduction to Women's and Gender Studies.[5] Two were sections taught over a traditional, sixteen-week semester, face-to-face. Two were taught in an accelerated, three-week session, one in January (offered online) and the other in May in a face-to-face format. We were interested in investigating three interconnected research questions:

- How does students' understanding of the four threshold concepts that structure WAGS 201 evolve and change over the course of the semester, as evidenced by their performance in course assessments?
- How is student learning in the course affected by what Meyer and Land call pre-liminal variation, defined as "variation in students' 'tacit' understanding (or lack thereof) of a threshold concept?" (2005, p. 384)
- What learning bottlenecks do students encounter in the introductory course, and what might be causing them?

To find the answers to these questions, we collected several types of evidence of student learning from the 72 student participants in our study:

- Three "Skills Assessments": essays written in response to take-home writing prompts that asked students to apply the threshold concept from the textbook to a new example or artifact. Skills Assessments (or SAs), were designed to get at students' understanding of the concepts of the social construction of gender, privilege and oppression, and intersectionality
- Final, reflective discussion posts: these included contributions and responses to a discussion prompt in our learning management system (LMS), D2L, asking students for a final reflection on the course

---

[4]See Meyer and Land (2003, 2005), Land et al. (2005, 2010, 2014), and Cousin (2007).
[5]The project, "Threshold Concepts in Women's and Gender Studies: A Study of Student Learning," received IRB approval from the University of Wisconsin Oshkosh (Protocol number: 973038).

- Reflective essay: this assignment was tied to the fourth threshold concept, feminist praxis, and as a reflective genre of writing is less intended to ask students to apply a lens or concept to a specific, provided example (such as other assessments that gave students video clips, ads, data, etc.) than it is to ask students to articulate their current thinking and application of the primary threshold concepts to contexts outside of the classroom.

We have turned to this rich source of data, artifacts of student learning, in order to shape this book. After creating an alphabetized spreadsheet of the 72 students in our study, we methodically made our way through the list. Over the course of approximately five months, we convened weekly via Skype after reading the work of three or four students. Prior to meeting every week, we made observations in a shared spreadsheet about each student's work in relation to each of our research questions. By the time we were about halfway through our list, we had started to notice several themes and trends, which prompted us to create another shared document where we noted them and began collecting examples that illustrated them. After reading and analyzing the texts of all of the participating students, we distilled the themes and trends into four key areas. Readers will see these themes woven into each of the book chapters:

1. **New Language**: Because our SoTL project focused on analyzing the written work of students, it is perhaps unsurprising that we came away believing that much of the heavy lifting performed by the introductory course has to do with introducing students to new academic language and giving them opportunities to incorporate that language into their repertoire, spoken and written. Meyer and Land note the discursive nature of threshold concepts and assert, "It is hard to imagine any shift in perspective that is not simultaneously accompanied by (or occasioned through) an extension of the students' use of language" (2005, p. 374). On one level, this means that students are introduced to key concepts of the field and asked to use them when engaging in class discussions and completing written assignments as a way of demonstrating understanding. For some students more than others, the discursive nature of these threshold concepts is a source of struggle, or "troublesomeness," as Meyer and Land have called it. As they note, "The discursive practices of a given community may render previously 'familiar' concepts strange and subsequently conceptually difficult" (2006, p. 14).

   On another level, this may mean considering the *implications* of course concepts for their language usage, e.g., using gender-neutral pronouns as a part of learning about the constructedness of the sex/gender binary. An increasing challenge is how to introduce students to "new language" that is not new to them. As gender studies concepts filter out and circulate through popular discourse (e.g., intersectionality, toxic masculinity, rape culture, privilege), students increasingly come into the Intro classroom feeling like they know what these terms mean and so sometimes understanding new language is first about *unlearning* what a student might have thought those terms meant. Especially when students have encountered course concepts through the fun-house mirror distortions of internet extremism, instructors will need to create space for unlearning as part of building a foundation for understanding new language.

2. **Divergent Entry Points**: We included a research question about pre-liminal variation in this SoTL project as a follow up from an earlier SoTL project that focused on student learning using a threshold concepts model for teaching introductory WGS.[6] In reading students' writing, we found that many of the students who struggled to cross the threshold of understanding for one or more of the concepts made clear, directly or indirectly, that they were encountering those concepts and frameworks for the first time, and that they were often not only new, but that they were "troublesome," in one or more ways, including that they ran counter to prior received knowledge.

Conversely, many of the students whose written work demonstrated advanced understanding of the threshold concepts revealed that they were building on prior knowledge that was acquired in another course and/or outside the classroom altogether. This group included students who indicated that their prior knowledge came at least in part from generating a critical analysis of their own identities and experiences as members of one or more marginalized groups. Our most recent SoTL project cemented our conviction that students' starting points significantly shape the trajectory of their learning in the introductory course.

Outside the context of our research project, this point about pre-liminal variation can also connect to the stage of their undergraduate career at which students take the course. Over the years, Susan and Christie taught many sections of Intro reserved for traditional-aged, first-semester students; the frame of reference for these students was their still-fresh experiences in high school. During the same period, Holly taught on a two-year campus that only offered first and second-year courses, though many of her students were non-traditional and returning adult students

---

[6] See Hassel and Launius (2017).

who brought with them a wide range of experiences between their secondary and postsecondary educations. Anecdotally, we have a sense that students encounter the course in general, and the course material and their classmates more specifically, in different ways depending on where they are at in their undergraduate career and the pathways that brought them to the intro course.

Yet another way to think about the divergent starting points of students in the introductory course is related to their academic preparedness more generally for college-level work. Students whose prior educational experiences were not aligned with the academic expectations of college often benefit from and deeply appreciate both the content of the introductory course as well as the principles of feminist pedagogy that guide it, though they may struggle more or differently with some course materials because of varying levels of past experience with critical reading tasks in their prior education. The fact that students start the course from divergent places has implications for course design, as well as choices about course materials and pedagogical activities, and it is important to keep these things in mind when designing assignments and assessing student work.

3. **Affective Learning**: A third theme that emerged from our analysis of our students' writing is the role—and the importance of—affective learning. By this we mean several things. First, one aspect of students' potential development or growth in the course is emotional, and part of students' learning processes in the course can be characterized as emotional labor, given that learning in WGS courses sometimes requires emotional vulnerability. Further, this emotional labor occurs both as a result of how each student responds to the course material, but also as a result of their interactions with classmates in the course. In addition, students' affective responses to course material and/or their classmates can serve as a pathway to further learning, as when a student is powerfully moved by a course reading and classroom discussion about it and is inspired to dig deeper, read more, and seek out additional perspectives; conversely, those affective responses can function as what Middendorf and Shopkow refer to as "emotional bottlenecks" (2018). This focus on affective learning links back to our discussion of pedagogies of invitation above; as instructors, we strive not just to listen to what our students are saying, whether in class discussions or their written work for the course, but also to try to hear and understand the affect that lies behind and animates their words. We aim to understand not just what they say but where it's coming from, affectively. Throughout this book, we discuss how pedagogical, course design, and instructional choices can support this kind of learning and

also how affective dimensions of learning can intersect with the cognitive load of absorbing new information and ideas in both useful and difficult ways. We think it's important for instructors to consider how to balance some of the dispositional and affective growth that socially engaged courses develop with the more traditional academic and "content" course outcomes. In "Threshold Concepts, Troublesome Knowledge, and Emotional Capital: An Exploration into Learning about Others," Glynis Cousin explores how the threshold concept of "Otherness" is taught in the field of Cultural Studies. She is interested in how students' subject positions shape their relationship to this particular threshold concept; more generally, she asserts that "learners will always be emotionally and socially positioned vis-a-vis whatever they are learning" (qtd. In Meyer and Land 2006, p.137). She explores whether and how a student's "experiential proximity" to concepts "*may* bring more emotional capital to their understandings of them" (p. 138). Cousin defines emotional capital as a "set of assets" that some students bring to learning about concepts such as Otherness, a set of assets that comes from experiential proximity, defined broadly not just as social positioning, but also including "family and school cultures, ethical sensibilities and political awareness" (p. 138).

4. **Macro Thinking**: This last theme has to do with whether and to what extent students, over the course of the term, were able to grasp the structural dimensions of systems of privilege and oppression. This struck us as a fundamental dividing line among the students, and during the analysis stage of our SoTL project, became a recurring point of discussion in our weekly meetings. Some students demonstrated clearly through their writing that they grasped that privilege and oppression are systemic, and not just experienced interpersonally at the level of individuals; furthermore, many of these students could then utilize that understanding and employ it as an analytical lens. Other students, however, experienced a major stumbling block around this issue; some could summarize and paraphrase these ideas as presented by authors that we read, but when asked to apply them and/or to offer their responses to and reflections on this framework, reverted to language that reinforced the role of individuals in perpetuating or challenging privilege and oppression. Given the centrality to the field of WGS of adopting a sociological imagination (to use C. Wright Mills' term), insight into the ease or difficulty with which students grasp this concept is important to have, from a teaching perspective.

All four of these themes have implications for all aspects of teaching the introductory course; in the chapters that follow, we'll focus on how these insights into student learning might shape everything from course design, to choice of teaching materials, and the design of assignments that assess student learning. To illustrate our points, we will be quoting from our students' written work, using pseudonyms that we assigned.

1.4   The Intro Course Today

Teaching the introduction to women's and gender studies course (and other socially engaged courses) at the start of the twenty-first century offers both exciting opportunities and challenges. Most notably, the proliferation of online social media-based communities (on Instagram, Tumblr, Tik-Tok, Discord, and Twitter) has had the effect of making feminist ideas more accessible and multimodal; many students' introduction to feminist issues is through a consciousness-raising process that happens earlier than college and with much more access to types of information that didn't exist in the twentieth century. The accessibility of feminist media through "web 2.0" methods that allow for self-creation, dissemination, and DIY multimedia work means that students who are interested in WGS topics can seek out, locate, and participate in conversations about intersectional feminist issues, an opportunity that exists in few traditional academic curricula in the K-12 setting. Further, topics of social justice continue to be relevant to legislative, current events, and popular culture conversations, which in turn makes the relevance of the field clear to students. Activist efforts toward social justice such as Black Lives Matter, LGBTQ and trans* visibility efforts in politics and popular culture, and Alexandria Ocasio-Cortez's demystification of the workings of political power continue to capture the attention of the public in the United States and globally, particularly young people. These days, a student in the Intro course is likely to have learned something about WGS concepts already from an influential transgender woman YouTuber (like Contrapoints), an intersex make-up influencer on Instagram, K-Pop fandoms on Twitter, or a social justice server on Discord. All of these things didn't exist more than a few decades ago, and for those of us who are old enough to remember the excitement of feminist print zines in the 1990s, these are amazing developments.

On the flip side, the context of higher education has in many ways become more challenging. Corporate and business-model approaches to higher ed are prominent, such as the use of contingent faculty and low-stability positions, and the heavy emphasis for some instructors on student feedback as a form of evaluating their teaching, which can have the effect of making instructors less willing or able to challenge students' preexisting belief systems for fear of negative reviews. An Association of American Colleges and Universities survey report explained that "institutions' top five concerns are financial constraints, diversity and inclusion, retention and completion, assessment of learning outcomes, and communicating the value of liberal education. Yet, efforts to restore public trust in the promise of liberal education and inclusive excellence are hampered by a prevailing national rhetoric that attempts to decouple higher education from the American dream" (2018, p. 4). The curriculum and pedagogy of socially engaged curricula can be particularly challenging within this climate.

By the same token, this eroding public confidence in higher education has particular relevance for socially engaged interdisciplines like WGS because of the powerful rhetorics that circulate around the alleged liberal bias of college. The rise of the alt-right and its close connections to men's rights activists have created an increasingly hostile, and sometimes dangerous, campus climate for instructors of courses that examine gender, race, and sexuality. Some universities have fired or suspended instructors after, for example, being pressured by conservative alumni, and women's and gender studies instructors can face particular challenges in their courses. Barbara Ransby, past president of the National Women's Studies Association, notes "Our classrooms are a part of the larger society, and the kinds of divisions that exist and the kinds of scapegoating that exist spill over into our classrooms…It shouldn't be surprising that a number of our colleagues around the country have experienced hostility" (Kerr 2018).

Detractors of higher ed take a multi-pronged approach to cultivate mistrust of the goals of liberal arts education, and social justice-oriented disciplines in particular (as well as those in the humanities and social sciences more broadly). These include, for example, accusations that such courses are luxuries and do not support career-oriented goals that many students enter college with (or for traditional-age students, the goals their parents may have in selecting a college). The use of disparaging terms like "snowflakes" are popular among conservative critics and used to designate students who express resistance or make demands of the university, such as the story of Everett Piper, the president of a small evangelical Christian college, Oklahoma Wesleyan University, who responded to students that expressed discomfort with a campus sermon with his own viral letter, "This is Not a Day Care! It's a University" (Holohan 2017). Promoted by the right-wing media ecosphere, the language of equity has been parlayed into the language of critique, as the Collins English Dictionary more palatably defines the term "snowflake":

"The young adults of the 2010s, viewed as being less resilient and more prone to taking offence than previous generations" (Yagoda 2016). Higher education theorists and teachers have responded by pointing to the actual resilience of the students they teach, documenting the cultural, institutional, and financial milieux that are fundamentally different for Millennial and Gen Z students. *Salon* columnist David Masciotra writes, "My college students aren't 'snowflakes' — they're tougher than their critics could imagine" (2016). He rejects what he calls the "media caricature" of the modern college student by recounting the myriad challenges his students face such as caregiving responsibilities, part-time and full-time jobs aside from college, health and financial issues, among other extra-academic priorities.

Other considerations include the context for teaching rather than the students themselves. Not uncommon are media stories that appropriate terms like "safe spaces" and "trigger warnings" where students and faculty are labeled "social justice warriors." Such efforts initially emerged as a way of recognizing the increasing diversification of higher education with students other than from white, middle-class, cis, able-bodied, and other mainstream backgrounds now becoming predominant as the demographics of college-going populations change. The University of Chicago made headlines in 2016 when a letter to freshman from the dean of students, John Ellison announced the institution's rejection of these concepts: "Our commitment to academic freedom means that we do not support so-called 'trigger warnings,' we do not cancel invited speakers because their topics might prove controversial, and we do not condone the creation of intellectual 'safe spaces' where individuals can retreat from ideas and perspectives at odds with their own" (Grieve 2016). A columnist in the *Chronicle of Higher Education* called on "free speech" to have its own "safe space": "It is speech that must enjoy the safe zone, both within the collective of the class and within the individual student," linking calls for safe spaces to efforts to limit free speech (Gup 2016). As WGS classrooms often aim to create a learning environment in which students can participate in discussions of challenging ideas while also being assured that efforts are made to ensure bigotry of whatever nature is unwelcome as part of those discussions, WGS instructors can find themselves particularly targeted by ideologues. Content warnings, as well, intended to help those students (or colleagues for that matter) be able to anticipate potentially retraumatizing topics, texts, and images (in order to give students agency over how they experience them), are not unusual in WGS courses where content may include sexual violence, domestic violence, racist police brutality, or any other issue that may have difficult emotional resonance for students.

A parallel effort at work nationally is the freedom of expression movement, typified by resolutions and policies passed at trustee or administrative levels and intended to curb student and faculty activism around hate speech. This has taken a number of forms, all of which may have specific implications for teaching general-education socially engaged courses. The *Chronicle of Higher Ed* regularly reports on efforts by conservative lawmakers to pass "free speech bills" that are intended to ensure what they call "intellectual diversity." Appropriating the language of freedom of expression and diversity and inclusion, the legislative fixes are often derived from model policy created by conservative think tanks that "prevents the disinvitation of speakers, establishes penalties for those who interfere with speech, enables legal recourse for those whose rights have been violated, requires colleges to stay neutral on controversial public-policy questions, and requires a yearly report on free-speech issues on campus, among other things" (McMurtrie 2017). These efforts leave those who teach in socially engaged fields concerned about some of the repercussions that may emerge from their classroom work. For example, Turning Point USA, a right-wing organization established in 2012 to promote conservatism on college campuses, created a so-called "Professor Watchlist" that asks students to report on faculty they perceive to have a "liberal bias," or as *Inside Higher Ed* reported: "A new website is asking students and others to 'expose and document' professors who 'discriminate against conservative students, promote anti-American values and advance leftist propaganda in the classroom'" (Flaherty 2016). Faculty have appeared on the list not just for in-class discussion topics or readings but because of public positions such as newspaper columns they have written on political topics (Reilly 2016; Knott 2016), areas of research (Flaherty), or social media activities (Reilly). As such initiatives have gained traction, they can have a chilling effect on the willingness or ability of faculty in socially engaged fields to explore topics they perceive students will find too political or controversial.

As of spring 2020 and the onset of the global pandemic, the technology-mediated options for instruction create new opportunities for surveillance as well as access, with implications that have yet to be fully realized. More or even most college professors transitioned instruction from traditional face-to-face synchronous classrooms to emergency remote or planned online instruction, presenting new pedagogical challenges: for example, how to create the kinds of transformative learning experiences we hope for in socially engaged classrooms within a distance learning environment, and how to bridge the persistent digital divide that reinforces racialized economic inequality. Likewise, there is new potential emerging for online classrooms: asynchronous and remote instructional models may also increase the number of college students who can access courses, whether because of limited options in their own contexts or because they live in under-resourced rural or urban locations.

1.5   Who Students Are Now

Though narratives of entitlement and Millennial and Gen Z character deficiencies are easily found in the news and online, in actuality, the students in our classrooms are more diverse than ever, and few fit the parameters of the "snowflake" stereotype that is touted in the popular media. Demographically, the notion of a traditional college student—one who is middle-class, White, fresh from high school, 18 years old, and lives on-site at a four-year campus—reflects fewer and fewer students' realities. For example, according to the National Center for Education Statistics, around 19.7 million students attended college and universities in Fall 2020, and 5.8 million of those were enrolled at two-year college campuses, which are largely commuter schools. In this sense, many of today's college students are not spending four, consecutive years in a dorm or residential setting. Most students work: in 2018, 43% of undergraduate students worked jobs aside from school, though 78% of part-time undergraduates held jobs (45% of part-time students worked 35 or more hours per week, with 10% of full-time students working 35 or more hours per week) (McFarland et al. 2018).

Just over half of college students in the United States, according to the National Center for Educational Statistics, identify as white; students of color make up 44% of the college-going student population (NCES). As of 2015–2016, 24% of college students were the first in their families to attend college, and over half of all college students (56%) had parents without bachelor's degrees (RTI International). These first-generation students are more likely to attend two-year campuses; according to the Postsecondary National Policy Institute, "53% of first-generation students enrolled in a two-year institution, compared with 39% of students whose parents had at least a bachelor's degree." First-generation students are also more likely to attend college part-time; this more diverse student population faces significant educational barriers, as the First Generation Foundation notes: "Only 11% of low-income, first-generation college students will have a college degree within six years of enrolling in school, compared to about 55% of their more advantaged peers who were not low-income or first-generation students, according to a Pell Institute study of students who first enrolled in fall 2003" ("First-Generation" 2018). There is also a not-insignificant number of undergraduate student veterans. Approximately 4% of college students have served in the armed forces, and such students are most likely to be registered in public two-year and private for-profit colleges (American Council of Education 2015).

We note this increasing level of diversity in background, experience and demographics to emphasize the changing shape of WGS instruction and how this vibrant diversity calls us to ensure that our curriculum, pedagogy, and assessment of our students' learning is effective and responsive to changing student populations. Though he is writing about the field of Queer Studies rather than Women's and Gender Studies, we find Matt Brim's question, in his recent book *Poor Queer Studies: Confronting Elitism in the University*, provocative for our work here:

> [H]ow can rethinking the work of Queer Studies in the context of students' relative material need and raced/gendered precarity, academics' professional liminality, and underclass institutional identity inform and potentially enrich the field, its pedagogies, and theories, and the academy beyond it? (2020, p. 3)

We circle back here to our earlier point about the importance of considerations of the local when approaching the introductory course, and add to it that we may need to question whether and to what extent we have internalized notions of who college students are based on the ideological constructions that circulate in a variety of discourses. As instructors who have spent the vast majority of our careers in decidedly non-elite institutions, we are also keen to dispute the notion that students at such institutions are less interested in or more resistant to the ideas and arguments in introductory WGS courses.

1.6   How to Use This Book

The primary aim of this book is to provide, within this context, a practical and evidence-based guide to instructors preparing to teach (or who are revising and rethinking) an introductory Women's and Gender Studies (WGS) course, with a particular focus on the kinds of course materials and classroom experiences that promote student learning, and the assessment practices that can provide instructors feedback on whether, what, and to what extent, students are learning. As such, this book joins a long tradition of writing about feminist pedagogy in general, and the introductory course in particular.

However, what *A Guide to Teaching Introductory Women's and Gender Studies: Socially Engaged Classrooms* does is move beyond the sharing of ideas and teacher narratives to (1) equip instructors with key principles for approaching the classroom, distilled from research that is systematically collected and the product of structured inquiry; and (2) provide a practical guide for designing or redesigning the introductory WGS course that helps instructors adapt their pedagogy to a range of classroom environments as well as anticipate the emotional, intellectual, and interpersonal challenges and rewards of teaching and learning in the introductory WGS course. In this book, readers will find invitations to reflect, support for metacognitive activities, and self-assessment tools to help new instructors articulate their goals and values as they approach course design.

Chapter 2 focuses on principles for crafting the course and makes the case for starting that process by intentionally and explicitly considering a range of possible learning outcomes. Chapter 3 builds on a consideration of learning outcomes by raising a number of issues related to choosing course materials and considering pedagogical activities that help students work toward the chosen learning outcomes. Chapter 4 then turns to designing and evaluating assessments of students' learning. Finally, Chapter 5 presents sample syllabi and assignments with annotations that provide explanations of the rationale for each of the choices made in the assignment design.

We offer an additional note in the context of drafting this manuscript in 2020, in the midst of the COVID-19 global pandemic. We intend for this book to be relevant for a range of delivery modes and course lengths. The book itself addresses and is built on a foundation of research and experience teaching online, asynchronous WGS courses (see Chick and Hassel 2009). This thinking suffuses the chapters, even before the pandemic compelled a majority of teachers to become familiar with non-face-to-face teaching modalities. The book is intended to support instructors' course design and pedagogy in multiple contexts—needed now more than ever before.

Works Cited

American Council on Education. 2015. By the numbers: Undergraduate student Veterans. *ACENET*. https://www.acenet.edu/the-presidency/columns-and-fea tures/Pages/By-the-Numbers-Undergraduate-Student-Veterans.aspx. Accessed 16 January 2021.

Association of American Colleges and Universities. 2018. 2018–2022 strategic plan: Educating for democracy. AAC&U. https://www.aacu.org/sites/default/files/files/about/AACU_StrategicPlan_2018-22.pdf. Accessed 16 January 2021.

Brim, Matt. 2020. *Poor queer studies: Confronting elitism in the university*. Durham: Duke University Press.

Calder, Lendol. 2006. Uncoverage: Toward a signature pedagogy for the history survey. *The Journal of American History* 92: 1358–1370.

Chick, Nancy, and Holly Hassel. 2009. 'Don't hate me because I'm virtual': Feminist pedagogy in the online classroom. *Feminist Teacher* 19: 195–215.

Cousin, Glynis. 2007. Exploring threshold concepts for linking teaching and research. Paper presented to the International Colloquium: International Policies and Practices for Academic Enquiry. https://www.ee.ucl.ac.uk/~mflanaga/Glynis_Cousin_Exploring_.pdf. Accessed 16 January 2021.

Denial, Catherine. 2020. A pedagogy of kindness. In *Critical Digital Pedagogy: A Collection*, ed. Jesse Stommel, Chris Friend, and Sean Michael Morris, 212–218. Washington, DC: Hybrid Pedagogy, inc.

First-generation students. 2018. Postsecondary National Policy Institute. http://pnpi.org/first-generation-students/. Accessed 16 January 2021.

Flaherty, Colleen. 2016. Being watched. *Inside Higher Ed*, November 22. https://www.insidehighered.com/news/2016/11/22/new-website-seeks-register-professors-accused-liberal-bias-and-anti-american-values. Accessed 16 January 2021.

Gannon, Kevin M. 2020. *Radical hope: A teaching manifesto*. Morgantown: West Virginia University Press.

Grieve, Pete. 2016. University to freshmen: Don't expect safe spaces or trigger warnings. *The Chicago Maroon*, August 24. https://www.chicagomaroon.com/2016/08/24/university-to-freshmen-dont-expect-safe-spaces-or-trigger-warnings/. Accessed 16 January 2021.

Gup, Ted. 2016. A different kind of safe space. *The Chronicle of Higher Education*, August 30. https://www.chronicle.com/article/A-Different-Kind-of-Safe-Space/237625. Accessed 16 January 2021.

Hassel, Holly, and Christie Launius. 2017. Crossing the threshold in introductory women's and gender studies courses: An assessment of student learning. *Teaching and Learning Inquiry* 5: 30–46.

Hill, Catherine. 2013. Classrooms of justice: Teaching gender studies in grades 7–12. *AAUW*, August 27. https://www.aauw.org/article/teaching-gender-studies/. Accessed 16 January 2020.

Hobbs, Margaret, and Carla Rice. 2012. Rethinking women's studies: Curriculum, pedagogy, and the introductory course. *Atlantis: Critical Studies in Gender, Culture, and Social Justice* 35: 139–149.

Holohan, Meghan. 2017. 'Not a daycare': College president says 'snowflake' student problem persists. *Today*, August 9. https://www.today.com/parents/Not-daycare-college-president-calls-out-snowflakes-t102226. Accessed 16 January 2021.

Knott, Katherine. 2016. What it's like to be named to a watch list of 'American Professors'. *The Chronicle of Higher Education*, November 23. https://www.chronicle.com/article/What-It-s-Like-to-Be-Named/238486. Accessed 16 January 2021.

Keating, AnaLouise. 2013. *Transformation now! Toward a post-oppositional politics of change*. Urbana: University of Illinois Press.

Kerr, Emma. 2018. For scholars of women's studies, it's been a dangerous year. *Chronicle of Higher Education*, February 11. https://www.chronicle.com/article/for-scholars-of-womens-studies-its-been-a-dangerous-year/. Accessed 16 January 2021.

Kim, Crystal, and Jessica Ringrose. 2018. 'Stumbling upon: Teenage girls' forays into digital and school-based feminisms. *Girlhood Studies* 11: 46–62.

Land, Ray, Glynis Cousin, Jan H.F. Meyer, and Peter Davis. 2005. Threshold concepts and troublesome knowledge (3): Implications for course design and evaluation. In *Improving student learning: Diversity and inclusivity*, ed. Chris Rust. Oxford: Oxford Centre for Staff and Learning Development.

Land, Ray, J.H.F. Meyer, and Caroline Baillie. 2010. Editors' preface: Threshold concepts and transformational learning. In *Threshold Concepts and Transformational Learning*, eds Ray Land, JHF Meyer, and Caroline Bailiie, Ix–xlii. Rotterdam, Netherlands: Sense Publishers.

Land, R., J. Rattray, and P. Vivian. 2014. Learning in the liminal space: A semiotic approach to threshold concepts. *Higher Education*. Available on-line to journal subscribers. https://doi.org/10.1007/s10734-013-9705-x.

Launius, Christie, and Holly Hassel. 2018. *Threshold concepts in women's and gender studies: Ways of seeing, thinking, and knowing*. New York: Routledge.

Masciotra, David. 2016. My college students aren't snowflakes: They're tougher than their critics could imagine. *Salon*, December 19. https://www.salon.com/2016/12/19/My-college-students-arent-snowflakes-theyre-tougher-than-their-critics-could-imagine. Accessed 17 January 2021.

McFarland, J., et al. 2018. *The condition of education*. National Center for Education Statistics, May 23. https://nces.ed.gov/pubsearch/pubsinfo.asp?pubid=2018144.

McMurtrie, Beth. 2017. Why conservative lawmakers are turning to free-speech bills as a fix for higher ed. *The Chronicle of Higher Education*. https://www-chronicle-com.ezproxy.lib.ndsu.nodak.edu/article/Why-Conservative-Lawmakers-Are/240297. Accessed 17 January 2021.

Merlin, Michelle. 2017. Saucon Valley would be on cutting edge with gender studies course. *The Morning Call*, March 21. https://www.mcall.com/news/local/saucon-valley/mc-gender-studies-explained-saucon-valley-20170316-story.html. Accessed 17 January 2021.

Meyer, Jan, and Ray Land. 2003. Threshold concepts and troublesome knowledge: Linkages to ways of thinking and practising within the disciplines. Edinburgh: University of Edinburgh, *ETL Project*, Occasional Report 4.

———. 2005. Threshold concepts and troublesome knowledge (2): Epistemological considerations and a conceptual framework for teaching and learning. *Higher education* 49: 373–388.

———. 2006. *Overcoming barriers to student understanding: Threshold concepts and troublesome knowledge*. New York: Routledge.

Middendorf, Joan, and Leah Shopkow. 2018. *Overcoming student learning bottlenecks: Decode the critical thinking of your discipline.* Sterling, VA: Stylus.

Olwan, Dana, AnaLouise Keating, Catherine M. Orr, and Beverly Guy Sheftall. 2016. Make/shift pedagogies: Suggestions, provocations, and challenges for teaching introductory gender and women's studies courses. *Atlantis* 37: 8–21.

Pew Social Trends. 2019. Gen Z more familiar with gender-neutral pronouns, January 14. https://www.pewsocialtrends.org/2019/01/17/generation-z-looks-a-lot-like-millennials-on-key-social-and-political-issues/psdt_1-17-19_generations-03/. Accessed 17 January 2021.

Postsecondary Public Policy Institute. 2020. First-generation students in higher education, November 6. https://pnpi.org/wp-content/uploads/2020/11/FirstGenStudentsinHigherEd_November2020-FINAL.pdf. Accessed 8 January 2021.

Reilly, Katie. 2016. Professors targeted by conservative watchlist fire back: It's obviously an attempt to silence people. *Time*, December 1. http://time.com/4588165/professor-watchlist-silence-conservative/. Accessed 17 January 2021.

RTI International. 2019. *First-generation college students: demographic characteristics and postsecondary enrollment.* Washington, DC: NASPA. https://firstgen.naspa.org/files/dmfile/FactSheet-01.pdf. Accessed 8 January 2021.

Table 306.20: total fall enrollment in degree-granting postsecondary institutions, by level and control of institution and race/ethnicity of student: selected years, 1976–2017. 2018. Digest of Education Statistics. *National Center for Education Statistics.* https://nces.ed.gov/programs/digest/2018menu_tables.asp. Accessed 17 January 2021.

White, Melissa Autumn, and Jennifer Musial. 2016. Inspired reflections: An introduction. *Atlantis: Critical Studies in Gender, Culture, and Social Justice* 37: 3–7.

Yagoda, Ben. 2016. Who you calling snowflake? *The Chronicle of Higher Education*, December 4. https://www.chronicle.com/blogs/linguafranca/2016/12/04/who-you-calling-snowflake/. Accessed 8 January 2021.

2

Principles for Crafting Your Course and Classroom Environment

As Holly and Christie have written about elsewhere (see Hassel and Launius 2017), our approach to teaching the introductory course has evolved over time, and most notably, as a result of ongoing conversations over the course of almost a decade with colleagues across a wide range of institutions in the University of Wisconsin System. It was in the context of the Women's and Gender Studies Consortium that the three of us were introduced to the framework of threshold concepts and began thinking about how that framework might be useful for understanding student learning in the field of Women's and Gender Studies, and in the introductory course in particular. The paths that each of us took to teaching Intro differ significantly and have shaped both how we continue to teach it today and our interest in studying student learning in it.

Holly: My graduate coursework in women's literature and accompanying familiarity with feminist theory and feminist literary criticism was one foundation that I brought to a faculty position at the University of Wisconsin-Marathon County, an open-admissions two-year campus in a small city in central Wisconsin. Though I was hired largely for my generalist background in both composition and rhetoric and literary studies, my interest in feminist activism and theory led to an invitation from our institution's online program director to develop an online-only version of our introductory course, one that served a range of students throughout the state, largely non-traditional student populations as well as students with varying levels of academic preparation.

© The Author(s), under exclusive license to Springer Nature
Switzerland AG 2021
H. Hassel et al., *A Guide to Teaching Introductory Women's and Gender Studies*,
https://doi.org/10.1007/978-3-030-71785-8_2

As a total newcomer to the field proper, I had the somewhat unusual experience of designing an online course from scratch and also teaching the course itself for the first time. Online courses at the UW Colleges were set up in toto at the start of the semester, so designing each unit and working with an instructional designer from our online program office meant that I had to start at least from organizing principles and with assessments of student learning that were spelled out in a compatible way with the expectations of the program, including breaking the course down into units of study and identifying learning outcomes for each unit as well as for the course as a whole (see Chick and Hassel 2009).

In this way, I have, from the outset of my instructional work in WGS, been focused on learning outcomes, but the shift has been from content to concept. My earliest efforts emerged largely from the textbook I selected, *Women: Images and Realities,* which was structured around topics and included excerpts from classic and contemporary writing to support students' understanding of those topics. Like many instructors, I also supplemented each unit's focus of study with related readings about current events or popular culture. Eventually, I began offering a section of the class in a face-to-face format on our small campus, and because the institutional mission was access rather than selectivity, the course included students with a very wide range of academic preparation, personal experiences, and backgrounds.

I started to recognize the ways that a "content" or "topic-only" version didn't necessarily help me make the core ideas of the course clear to student. When I shifted to Shaw and Lee's *Women's Voices, Feminist Visions* textbook for both my online and F2F sections, I saw the clear value of one of the early chapters on "Systems of Privilege and Oppression" was to helping students get at the big ideas that I was interested that they leave with as learners. For me, two professional experiences were turning points in helping me move to a threshold concepts approach, one that distilled what the key ways of thinking, seeing, and knowing in the field were. One was my increasing involvement with our Women's Studies Consortium, a system-wide group of WGS directors and chairs who met twice annually. When I became chair of the UW Colleges Women's and Gender Studies department (our 13-campus institution made up of small, two-year campuses throughout the state), I also began attending the Consortium meetings. Since our entire focus as two-year campuses was on *transfer* (94% of our students identified in the CCSSE survey that they intended to go on for a four-year degree), I had always had to think very intentionally about what students needed as a foundation to be able to move on to their next destination; at the Consortium, this meant thinking about what the common learning goals were at our Intro course level, since at least some of our students then took that foundation with them to more advanced courses in the discipline.

The second significant factor for me in moving to a disciplinary way of knowing approach was the work some colleagues in our program began doing on threshold concepts, and collaborative efforts around our program's assessment goals, including creating an assessment activity around the threshold concept we called "patriarchy as a system" (which we later published in a Scholarship of Teaching and Learning journal; see Hassel et al. 2011). Moving our thinking to outcomes that didn't just focus on "knowing" but also on "thinking like" ultimately transformed my pedagogical approaches and my thinking as a disciplinary teacher-scholar.

Christie: When I developed and taught my first Intro course as a master's level graduate student in the mid-1990s in what was then called Women's Studies, my strategy for doing so entailed borrowing liberally from the syllabus of the established professor whose class I had been a teaching assistant for in previous semesters. I had no notion of course planning beyond choosing topics and assigning readings, and I relied heavily on the textbook I adopted in making those choices. I proceeded along in this vein, gaining experience over the years and developing notions of what worked and what didn't in terms of topics, readings, assignments, etc.

Starting in 2004, my approach to Intro shifted substantially as I stepped into an administrative role directing a WS program with a minor. Like many small programs, the Intro course was the only core, required course; the remainder of the minor consisted of cross-listed courses based in a range of humanities and social science disciplines. As such, I began thinking about the course not just as a self-contained unit, but as a part of the program's curriculum, and more specifically a crucial, foundational part of it. My aim in teaching the Intro course at that institution was to introduce key concepts and a theoretical framework that students could carry forward into a range of disciplinary contexts as they completed the minor.

My approach to teaching Intro shifted again in 2008, when I became Director of an undergraduate program that was revising its learning outcomes upon the occasion of launching a new undergraduate major in Women's Studies (which was renamed Women's and Gender Studies in 2013). This was my first introduction to student learning outcomes, and I found the framework really helped me develop the thinking that had begun in my previous program, as it helped me be explicit as an instructor, both to myself and to the students, about the learning goals of the course, and it also aided my thinking about the relationship between the Intro course and the larger curriculum of which it was a part.

My narrative intersects with Holly's, as I too participated in the meetings of the University Wisconsin System Women's Studies Consortium, and participated in intense and ongoing conversations with my colleagues across the UW System about student learning in the introductory course.

Susan: I taught the Intro course for the first time in 2009. I was a new tenure-track joint hire in Women's and Gender Studies and History at a four-year comprehensive university that had just launched a major in Women's and Gender Studies. I had previously taught primarily history courses, where my training in gender and sexuality studies was certainly evident but not in the forefront. At my previous institution, I was a member of the Women's Studies affiliate faculty and had also spent a semester as Interim Director of the Women's Studies program while a faculty member was on sabbatical. Since my Ph.D. training in the history of science and medicine was also very interdisciplinary and included feminist studies and science studies, I was already comfortable outside of disciplinary lines, but my preparation for the Intro course was still a steep learning curve. I used a textbook-reader that employed a topics-based approach to the Intro course. Throughout the semester, we moved through topics like "Media" and "Social Policy" and "Religions." The readings were a bit hit and miss; we had some really great classroom discussions and, if I'm being honest, at least one really awful one when two students started yelling at each other about the Bible. I was by this point a fairly experienced instructor, but I had not yet fully honed my teaching persona for the Intro to WGS classroom.

Most of the assignments for the course were mandated by the Women's and Gender Studies program, but I developed a student blog assignment, which was a great source of student engagement over the years until internet trolling on Tumblr took the fun out of it. In terms of assessment of student learning, the blog was a space to track student learning over time and also to measure their civic engagement with the world around them. The other assignments were ostensibly connected to learning outcomes, but over time I started to feel like I was mostly just assessing them based on writing and analysis quality, which wasn't always a reflection of student learning of course concepts. I was eager to adopt a threshold concepts approach when my program started to move in that direction. Once I made the transition to the threshold concepts approach, I immediately saw the benefits to student learning because I became more intentionally focused on core concepts in ways that made the fundamental building blocks of the course legible to students.

We offer our diverse journeys to the Intro course here in order to illustrate just a few of the pathways to teaching it, and as a reminder that many come to teaching it well after graduate school. More generally, though this has been changing slowly over time, we know that many university faculty begin teaching full-time after graduate school without the benefit of studying course design, pedagogy, or assessment as part of their graduate curriculum, even in their home disciplines. In this chapter, we provide a heuristic for determining learning goals for your Intro course, as well as making choices about curriculum, and pedagogical approaches that can help you design a course that works for you and your students.

2.1 Principles of Design and Questions for Consideration

When designing or revising an introductory course, we recommend beginning by posing and answering the following question: "What do you want students to know, and what do you want them to be able to do, as a result of completing your course?" More specifically, we advocate *starting* with student learning outcomes and choosing course materials, assignments, and classroom activities that support those outcomes, rather than the other way around. For example, it is tempting for instructors to start from the point of what they want to do, what they want students to read—focusing more on the activities they'd like students to *do* in class and the readings that they find important. Without a clear and obvious focus on end goals, however, teaching can veer into a succession of vaguely related topics and readings when courses should be a strategically sequenced set of activities in the service of learning outcomes.

Learning outcomes, therefore, are the foundation of your course design—they will help you identify the big picture learning goals for the course, and what students should be able to do or know after they complete the course. As you begin thinking about the learning goals for your course, we also suggest that you do so in light of what you know about the student population at your institution. Below are some questions to consider, as well as suggestions for gathering up relevant information:

- Who is the student population at your campus or institution? Institutions often have this information available under links like "Fast Facts" or "Institutional research" or sometimes "Fact Book." You can learn more about the demographics and preparation of the student population that might help you get a clearer picture of the students the campus serves. Some information that might be helpful is to learn about the demographic breakdown in terms of gender, race, age, socioeconomic status, and/or first-generation status. Are students largely from the surrounding community or is it a "destination" school that is residential and attracts students from a national pool? Is it selective academically or open-admission? Do students live on campus or do the majority commute to campus?

- Talk with colleagues and chairs of other programs who can give you some insight into the typical students who are attracted to the program and/or why they might be enrolling in the course.
- Ensure that you understand the curricular purpose of the class and what students' motivation for registering for it might be. Does it fulfill a requirement for a particular major or for the general-education program? Is it a requirement for the minor or major in the field? Having a grasp of what students might be bringing to the course in terms of their educational goals can help you customize the course learning goals and outcomes. For example, does your institution have a strong focus on the health sciences, e.g., nursing, public health, etc.? If so, are there ways you could tailor or customize your course to directly address issues of concern (e.g., social determinants of health, horizontal segregation in allied health occupations, etc.) to students in those programs?

Knowing about the students who are in your classroom is an important step toward designing effective learning experiences that will meet student needs and make for a meaningful and engaging learning experience.

The language of course-level and program/department-level learning outcomes is fairly ubiquitous in higher education in the twenty-first century. A quick glance reveals that most WGS programs and departments have posted student learning outcomes on their websites, and sometimes information about how those learning outcomes are assessed at a programmatic level. Articulating course-level student learning outcomes is important for a number of reasons. First and foremost, the practice of articulating student learning outcomes helps instructors be conscious of and intentional about what they would like students to learn in their courses. Stating the learning outcomes on the syllabus *and* integrating their language fully into the course also creates transparency for students, which is to say, it provides a shared context for students' learning in your class and helps demystify the instructor's expectations. Having fully integrated student learning outcomes also sets the stage for gauging whether and to what extent students have achieved those outcomes, using assessment tools of our own devising. We can also examine those assessments in order to glean feedback about our teaching, making changes and adjustments in order to enhance and strengthen student learning.

Explicitly articulating the learning outcomes for the course can also be a part of the process of making the case for how a course helps students meet university-level learning outcomes. Instructors can seek approval to have their course count for general-education requirements and receive specific designations within that curriculum. Put a different way, employing the framework of student learning outcomes can be helpful in demonstrating and making visible the fact that many teaching practices (e.g., civic engagement and high-impact educational practices, for example) that are currently fashionable in higher education are the longtime stock-in-trade of Women's and Gender Studies.

More broadly, having course-level student learning outcomes also sets the stage for thinking about student learning across multiple courses, and the place of the introductory course in the broader curriculum. For example, some student learning outcomes might appear in multiple courses across the curriculum, but with rising expectations in upper-level courses. Thinking in terms of the larger curriculum also helps programs/departments identify what learning outcomes should be included in the introductory course in order to begin the scaffolding process necessary to achieve higher-level learning in advanced courses.

Threshold concepts could come back into play in the context of thinking about learning outcomes for the introductory course as well. As described in Chapter 1, threshold concepts are considered a kind of portal—a way for new learners to unlock ways of seeing, thinking, and knowing in the field. The metaphor of the portal is meant to suggest that there are some concepts that a student has to have a base level of understanding of in order to go on to more advanced thinking and learning in that field. Threshold concepts frequently entail a paradigm shift in a learner.

We have sought to use an inductive approach, one that draws from our experiences teaching women's and gender studies to a diverse range of students, in order to both identify common challenges students face and surface what the core ways of thinking are in the discipline in hopes of creating a pathway for students into the field. In the context of this project, our aim is not to make a case for the particular threshold concepts that we have identified and organize our introductory courses around, but instead to prompt thinking and reflection on your own teaching and observations of student learning, and to think about what concepts should be at the center of your introductory courses (and therefore reflected in your course's learning outcomes) given their centrality to student learning.

2.2   Learning Outcomes

We offer here an overview of learning outcomes that are common in Women's and Gender Studies programs. These outcomes can be broadly, though messily, separated into **content-** and **skills-based** outcomes, and the skills-based outcomes can be further divided into categories focused on **analysis, dispositions/habits of mind, process**, and **praxis**.

Over the years, we have found two sources of information about student learning outcomes in Women's and Gender Studies courses and programs to be particularly helpful: Amy Levin's 2007 report for the National Women's Studies Association, "Questions for a New Century: Women's Studies and Integrative Learning," which both provides an overview of previous assessment efforts in the field from the 1970s onward and surveys "current assessment plans and mission statements at a variety of institutions," (p. 16) and Tracy Berger and Cheryl Radeloff's book *Transforming Scholarship: Why Women's and Gender Studies Students Are Changing Themselves and the World* (2015), which includes the results of a survey they conducted of 900 WGS graduates at 125 colleges and universities. One of the questions survey takers were asked to respond to was, "What is the most important concept that you learned in your undergraduate Gender and/or Women's Studies coursework?" **Content-Based Learning Outcomes**: Berger and Radeloff report that the five concepts mentioned most frequently by their survey respondents were: gender; intersectionality; inequality; equity; and empowerment. Levin's list is more expansive but covers similar ground, including the concept of privilege, and several of the listed concepts focus on knowledge and knowers, e.g., "gendered construction of knowledge," and "standpoint theory; importance of location; situated knowledge." As in many courses that draw from the social sciences and humanities bodies of knowledge, simply "knowing information"—whether the history of feminist movements or specialized vocabulary specific to the discipline—are a usual and necessary part of introducing students to the academic discipline.

Analytical Skills: The porousness between content- and skills-based learning outcomes quickly becomes apparent, as many of the content-based learning outcomes from above also appear as skills-based learning outcomes with reference to their application. For example, skills that commonly appear are "Using gender as a category of/for analysis," (Berger and Radeloff 2015, p. 166) and employing an intersectional analytical lens. Many skills-based learning outcomes used in WGS courses and programs are not unique to the field, but are instead found widely in the liberal arts. These include skills of critical thinking, reading, and analysis, as well as "constructing arguments with evidence obtained from research; an ability to engage in research and analysis in order to gather information to either support or refute concepts and ideas; [and] locating, evaluating, and interpreting diverse sources, including statistics" (Berger and Radeloff p. 166). Skills-based learning outcomes that assert the importance of applying knowledge to the world outside the classroom, and/or connecting knowledge gained in WGS courses with non-WGS coursework are very common as well, and dovetail nicely with the language of integrative learning, which the Association of American Colleges and Universities defines as "an understanding and a disposition that a student builds across the curriculum and co-curriculum, from making simple connections among ideas and experiences to synthesizing and transferring learning to new, complex situations within and beyond the campus." Analytical skills, then, can be framed both as those that have broad use across disciplines/courses, or those like "use gender as a category of analysis" with some discipline-specific use.

Our collective experience using the threshold concepts approach and analyzing student writing in our SoTL project has led us to bring a sharper focus to analysis skills. The field of Women's and Gender Studies, like other academic fields, has a specialized vocabulary and also employs particular types of analysis; we suggest making this explicit and transparent in the course learning outcomes. In our own teaching, we tend to hone in on whether and how well students are able to incorporate WGS-specific concepts and frameworks into their own thinking and writing. As instructors, we frequently gauge whether and to what extent students have acquired knowledge of a concept by asking them to apply their content knowledge in the service of analysis and/or action. This also means asking students to reflect on their own thinking, including what their prior understanding of the concept was, and how course activities have challenged, affirmed, or complicated their previous understanding. As we'll discuss in Chapters 3 and 4, there are a number of pedagogical and assessment strategies for building this kind of metacognitive learning goal into the course.

Dispositions or Habits of Mind: Some skills-based learning outcomes are less tangible, and can be characterized as dispositions or habits of mind. For example, Berger and Radeloff's list of skills includes "developing and cultivating openness, awareness, and respect of individuals, groups, perspectives, and experiences that may differ from their own" (Berger and Radeloff p. 166). We would include Cynthia Enloe's concept of feminist curiosity[1] under this heading, as well as empathy and perspective-taking. One way of thinking

---

[1]See Cynthia Enloe, *The Curious Feminist: Searching for Women in a New Age of Empire* (2004).

about this category of learning outcomes is that they enable and facilitate the acquisition of content-based learning outcomes in the field. For example, in "Empathy Education: Teaching about Women and Poverty in the Introductory Women's Studies Classroom," Jennifer Scanlon writes of turning to what she calls empathy education after becoming frustrated by students' responses to a unit on women and poverty in which students steeped in bootstraps ideology repeatedly invoked classist and racist stereotypes. She sought "an approach that would actually teach empathy rather than numbers, understanding rather than abstraction" (p. 8). The workshop she designed to teach the material on women and poverty asked small groups of students to create a budget for a fictional family living in poverty; the process of doing so encouraged students to personalize or put a face on poverty and to gain an appreciation of the difficult, if not impossible, choices faced by people living in poverty. This perspective-taking exercise, she writes, increases students' ability to engage the statistics on women and poverty and to gain a better understanding of the role of public policy and social change in improving their lives and life chances. Ultimately, she stresses the importance of "educating for empathy as well as for knowledge" (p. 9). While we encourage instructors to make dispositional outcomes a visible and transparent part of their courses, we would like to provide the caveat that it is imperative to consider the implications of pedagogical activities such as this one for the student population your institution serves. Poverty-simulation exercises can be fraught for a number of reasons, not only because they can presume that students do not already have first-hand experiences of poverty, but also because a temporary, simulated experience of poverty has limited capacity for creating understanding.[2] In Chapter 3, in the context of our discussion of choosing course materials, we offer some ideas about a different approach to cultivating perspective-taking.

These dispositions or habits of mind also connect to one aspect of affective learning that we introduced in Chapter 1. In the context of student learning outcomes, this might take the form of asking students to reflect on some of the emotional experiences they have while encountering WGS/socially engaged content. We also see openness, empathy, and curiosity as aspects of affective learning. Overall, we advocate for having a learning outcome related to affective/dispositional learning, and also thinking about how to assess that

---

[2]See Carreiro and Kapitulik's "Budgets, Board Games, and Make Believe: The Challenge of Teaching Social Class Inequality with Non-Traditional Students" for a thorough discussion of this type of classroom exercise and its limitations in the field of Sociology. They argue that simulation exercises "run the risk of being ineffective, alienating, and potentially ethically suspect" (232).

outcome by giving students opportunities to make their shifts in perspective (or lack thereof) visible.

Process Skills: When considering the integration of process skills into the introductory course, one place to start is by asking the question, "What skills do students need in order to function and participate as a part of the classroom community in this WGS course?" In "Teaching Feminist Process," Nancy Schneidewind advocates the teaching of "feminist process skills"; namely, "skills for: 1) communicating, 2) developing a democratic group process, 3) cooperating, 4) integrating theory and practice, and 5) creating change" (1987, p. 15) both within an individual course, and across an undergraduate major. In her discussion of the introductory course, she focuses on communication skills, and more specifically discusses identifying and distinguishing between thoughts and feelings, and giving constructive feedback. She argues that a focus on teaching feminist process skills is useful first and foremost because those skills are needed in classrooms run by instructors who employ techniques of feminist pedagogy. In other words, it is only fair to students that we as instructors model the processes that are built into our pedagogy and help students acquire them if we are going to have expectations about how students should work together and interact throughout the course. And in the context of the current discussion, it is therefore appropriate for these skills to be named explicitly among the course learning goals. We see these process skills as especially important in the context of creating a productive classroom space for discussing difficult and contentious issues across differences.

Schneidewind also discusses praxis as a feminist process skill, though she sees it as a "sophisticated" feminist process skill most appropriate for inclusion toward the end of the undergraduate major. **Praxis** as a skill/process-based learning outcome can also be seen as an extension of the concept of **integrative learning** discussed above, in that praxis can be understood as a particular form or kind of application of learning; in this case, application of learning toward the end goal of social transformation. Many courses and programs/departments have one or more learning outcomes that focus on praxis, though the language varies widely: action, activism, service learning, and civic engagement are all possible words and phrases in this type of learning outcome. In "Doing Feminist and Activist Learning Outcomes: What Should Students Be Able to Do as a Result of this Women's and Gender Studies Project/Course/Curriculum" (2011), Danielle DeMuth argues that if a WGS program/department wants to cultivate praxis-related skills in their undergraduate majors, it is not only appropriate but necessary to introduce those skills as a desired learning outcome in the introductory course. She argues that "If skills and knowledge for activism were identified and intentionally developed across the curriculum, individual assignments or courses in the curriculum would not bear the entire burden of teaching students how to change the world; rather, courses across the curriculum could build the necessary skills in preparation for other classes that focus on those skills needed for social transformation work" (p. 90). Of course, as we have previously acknowledged, most students who take the introductory course do not go on to become WGS majors, but that does not negate the desirability of incorporating a praxis-related learning outcome into subsequent general-education or major program courses. Demuth helpfully breaks her own praxis-related learning outcomes into four areas (critical consciousness, agency, research and theory, and critical reflection), and goes on to describe the readings, discussions, and assignments she uses in support of student learning in her introductory courses, as well as subsequent, more advanced WGS courses.

2.3   Crafting the Course: Course Design

In this section, we adapt some of the core principles of the well-established approach to instruction introduced in Wiggins and McTighe's *Understanding by Design* (1998), in part because one of our own early motivations in WGS teaching was the feeling of what writing studies scholar Ann Berthoff has called "all-at-onceness," (1990) that the range and significance of content and the learning dispositions we hoped to cultivate in our introductory courses all seemed so equally important that it was hard to figure out where to start. What *is* the most basic or foundational underpinning that will help students navigate a WGS course—ways of seeing, thinking, and knowing— and how can we design as purposefully as possible a learning experience that will support that work?

Building on the previous section in which you may have identified learning goals or course objectives in multiple areas (e.g., content knowledge, analysis skills, habits of mind, process skills, or praxis), you may be hoping for students to work toward many of those in multiple areas during the experience of a single course. But the truth is that cognitive load/overload should be factored into any course design, particularly because the information and perspectives offered in WGS can be new and possibly overwhelming for many students. In this way, it's important to use a process that can help you define what you want to prioritize and when. Wiggins and McTighe offer a number of heuristic tools for doing this kind of thinking. For example, they propose that instructors follow a three-step process as they imagine their courses:

1. Identify desired results
2. Determine acceptable evidence
3. Plan learning experiences and instruction

We like this set of directives because they can be used for big picture or smaller picture planning. You might ask what specific content knowledge you hope students will develop by the end of a course, and work back from the key learning outcomes. Likewise, you might identify a certain level of proficiency with analysis (of data, arguments, social phenomena, etc.), which could drive the design of a series of curricular experiences that will move students through and to the level of analysis you are expecting by the end of the course.

That being said, sometimes as an instructor, you'll need to consider how and whether the scaffolding (the notion of sequencing learning experiences, skills, activities, and assessments in a way that provides support for students' achievement of those learning goals) you're providing is sufficient to move students through a series of multiple kinds of substantive learning, and what you will use to assess how effectively students achieved those goals. We offer here an elaboration of some of the terms and concepts you need to keep in mind as you are planning your course, namely how your curriculum, pedagogical approach/learning activities, and assessment are aligned to help students achieve the learning goals for the course.

For example, curricular decisions might be those that you make as you think about the sequence in which you will introduce students to particular concepts, material, authors, or ways of thinking. The pedagogical decisions around the curriculum might include whether you plan to use lectures, small group discussions, large-group discussions, application activities, or some other way of introducing students to the material, like Scanlon's poverty workshop. The assessment piece would be to determine how and whether students have achieved the learning goal for the activity. For most instructors, at least some of the curriculum or assessment may be predetermined either by a departmental requirement or shared textbook selection. Such constraints will pre-determine at least part of what your choices may be in any of these three areas. For example, your program might determine that all sections will use open-educational resources, or that a common final project or exam is to be used by all instructors. Being aware of such parameters is important to making decisions about your course structure.

The key principle we emphasize here is coherence between the three areas: curriculum, pedagogy, and assessment in the service of course learning outcomes. We offer an example here. Let's say that one of your ultimate goals for the course is for students to develop process skills, analytical skills, and praxis. We would argue that students need exposure to multiple activities, content, and instruction that will develop those throughout the semester, which doesn't mean separate activities for each one but rather working to ensure that the overall pedagogical approach you use is giving students a lot of opportunities to practice in all those areas during each part of the class. For example, Holly's Intro course was offered in a recent semester as a four-week accelerated model, exclusively online, and yet she values the course outcomes related to praxis—asking students to take their learning outside of the class-room, to plan for and perform an act of feminist praxis. That might feel challenging in an online setting. Likewise, she wanted students to continue to develop their feminist process skills—collaboration, conversation, negoti-ating differences in perspectives, learning from others, as well as analytical skills in reading and analyzing complex texts. A course design that works toward these goals, particularly one that emphasizes backward design would start from the last unit of the course:

- Unit 4: Feminist Praxis: students select, design, and execute an Act of Feminist Praxis.
- Units 1–3: work to build the skills and knowledge required to achieve that final goal.

This means in terms of selecting methods for students to learn infor-mation, to practice collaborative knowledge building, and to apply course content to spaces outside the classroom, the instructor needs to ensure students are practicing all of that throughout the course. Holly's set-up has looked like this:

- Curriculum: students read a chapter from the textbook, along with supple-mental primary or secondary sources, data sets, or current events news stories.
- Pedagogy: Material is introduced by instructor notes and announce-ments at the start of the unit; students work exclusively in small groups with structured discussion prompts, receiving feedback and additional instructor direction throughout the activity.
- Assessment: short reading quizzes assess student understanding of the assigned material; class discussions are graded on a rubric that values engagement with peers, comprehension of material, and analysis and inquiry; unit reflection papers (2–3 pages) ask students to reflect on how

their thinking is evolving over the course of the unit, with direct references to not just the content but also the learning activities (small group discussions), and to make connections to their experiences and previous learning.

Across these three areas, students are asked to develop **content knowledge** by linking an assessment directly to readings, podcasts, and videos; **analytical skills** are cultivated by application exercises in the quizzes that ask not just for definitional understanding of key terms but also one or two questions for each quiz where students have to apply, say, the concept of class, race, or gender privilege to a specific, new piece of information or data. **Process skills** are practiced and assessed through graded discussions, while **metacognitive and affective skills** are practiced, taught, and assessed through instructor feedback on small group discussion engagement (over the course of the discussion), and in feedback on unit reflection papers (through a detailed rubric and narrative comments).

To work toward an activity, then, that asks students to engage in an "act of feminist praxis" is to ensure that they feel prepared to do so by having cultivated analysis, content knowledge, process, and metacognitive skills. It can be a risky, unfamiliar, or uncomfortable experience for students new to feminist thinking to identify a site and problem they want to tackle, even something relatively small and local like challenging a friend's sexist joke, contacting a company or local business about a problematic advertising campaign, or using social media to advocate for change. Without a reasonable foundation, and practice with, having these conversations, students will be unable to meaningfully and successfully complete a praxis activity. Aligning curriculum, pedagogy, and assessment in a coherent and cohesive way that works *toward* such skills is essential.

Another related note here (which we'll discuss further in Chapter 4) is attaching value in ways that are aligned with the stated course goals. By this, we mean ensuring that the weight attached to the different course activities is reflective of the stated values of the instructor. For example, in Holly's Intro to WGS course, 30% of the course grade was attached to weekly/unit-based small groups discussions, which included small group problem-solving or analysis tasks, and that were assessed overall for the students' participation in the week's discussion (not specifically by post number). Rubrics that assess multiple areas of discussion (reading comprehension, engagement with classmates, contribution to learning community, analysis of prompt or task) communicate to students that the discussion itself matters and is a core part of the course where learning takes place (rather than just one more writing assignment to be uploaded to the LMS for grading to earn a small number of points). This is one way to make sure the dialogic, interactive, and communal responsibility that accompanies it is valued and has both a pedagogical goal and accompanying value.

2.4   Cultivating a Teacherly Persona

During the course design (or redesign) process, we recommend reflecting on one's teacherly persona, which is to say, reflecting on how you would like to present yourself to students, and how you would like to position yourself in relation to them and to the course material. This persona is created through what Lesley Erin Bartlett calls "pedagogical performances," which not only consist of "embodied performances in the classroom," but also "performances of identity in documents such as syllabi, assignment sheets, and feedback on student work" (p. 92). Online or remote teaching contexts, particularly increasing during the COVID-19 global pandemic, call us to think even more intentionally about teacherly personas in a range of different contexts (whether completely asynchronous courses, remote instruction through videoconferencing, or a HyFlex model that uses multiple methods of engaging students). Crafting and refining your teacherly persona is a key component to understanding your role in the learning journey of students in the class.

One way to approach this task is by linking it to some of the choices made regarding process-based learning outcomes for the course. If, for example, feminist curiosity, perspective-taking, or the consideration of an issue from multiple perspectives are among the learning objectives for the course, these skills can and should be modeled by the instructor, a point echoed by James M. Lang, who argues in a *Chronicle of Higher Education* post that "our teaching personae should be consistent not only with our convictions about our discipline, but also with our classroom practices and the learning objectives we set for our students" (2007). At base, then, our teaching persona can be crafted around our intentional strategies for modeling some of the learning objectives for the course.

While this can be a good starting place, it is not the sum total of the considerations that go into crafting a teaching persona. Much has been written in the scholarship on feminist pedagogy about the ways in which students' fears, prejudices, hopes, and expectations come to be centered on the figure of the instructor, and how students' engagement with the course and course material is figured through the embodied presence of the instructor.[3] For example, Mel Michelle Lewis writes that "The ways in which my students understand my identities becomes part of the project as they sort out the complicated ideas of race, gender, sexuality, and class through the interpretation of course texts, including my own embodied text" (2011, p. 50). Susan observes that students often relate to her early on in a given semester by telling her that she reminds them of various funny, non-threatening, lesbian comics (she has gotten ostensibly complimentary comparisons to Ellen Degeneres, Tig Notaro, Cameron Esposito, Kate McKinnon, and Wanda Sykes all over the past decade). When students respond to her in that way, it provides a window into the ways that they are making meaning about who they think she is. It also reflects back how Susan's teaching persona (white lesbian mom who often dwells on the comically absurd contradictions of systems of inequality as a way to open up space for thinking differently) is being read (mostly) successfully. But it also reveals how much student schemas matter in making very early judgments about an instructor, and often, the Intro course by extension.

Student resistance can be especially acute for instructors who embody various forms of marginalized difference vis-a-vis their students, as when a Black instructor is teaching a class of predominantly white students, or when a queer, trans- or non-binary instructor is teaching a class of predominantly straight and cisgender students.[4] A different kind of student resistance can occur when an instructor *shares* key identities with majority group students but challenges students' expectations about what that means, as when a white instructor of primarily white students takes an explicitly anti-racist stance and foregrounds BIPOC authors' views. But in addition to resistance, instructors are frequently sought after and seen as role models, whether when students from underrepresented groups in higher education see their identities reflected in their instructor, or when an instructor presents themselves as an ally, accomplice, or co-conspirator to/with liberation struggles.

Part of this reflection on a teacherly persona, then, entails anticipating some of the ways that students are likely to see and respond to you (both consciously and unconsciously), and how that might shape or impact their learning in the course. The process of intentionally crafting a teacherly persona for introductory social justice-focused classes is arguably different

---

[3]See, for example, chapters by Duncomble, Bowleg, and Brokes and Twine in *Teaching Introduction to Women's Studies* and chapters by Sanchez-Casal, Hase, and Dorsey in *Twenty-First-Century Feminist Classrooms: Pedagogies of Identity and Difference* (2002).

[4]See Dawn Rae Davis, "Unmirroring Pedagogies" (2010) for a stark example of how this played out when she, a white U.S. woman, served as a graduate teaching assistant for professors who were South Asian and Chicana, and Debjani Chakravarty's article in *Teaching and Learning Inquiry* on pedagogical approaches to global diversity courses.

than when doing so for courses that students perceive (however erroneously) as politically neutral.

Another consideration entails thinking about how one's teacherly persona might change over time, as we age, and the distance between our age and that of traditional-age students widens. Depending on the institutional context and a given group of students, being relatively close in age to one's students can be an asset, a liability, or both. It can be an asset if students see the instructor as someone who can more easily relate to them and their generational point of view, but it can be a liability if students see the instructor as someone lacking in knowledge and authority because of their relative youth. A wider age difference can also factor in in complicated ways; on the one hand, it can potentially be easier to establish one's epistemic authority, but students might see older instructors as being out of touch or unaware of contemporary culture. In both cases, age intersects with other aspects of identity in complicated and sometimes unpredictable ways to shape how students see and respond to us as instructors. We see this as a particular consideration for the Intro course, which is often framed around issues of prominence in popular culture and youth culture.

For example, when Susan started teaching, she was keen to generate goodwill with traditional-age students by being conversant in their cultural reference points. Over time, she not only had trouble keeping up, but her teacherly persona also organically shifted where she instead said some version of the following to students: "I'm not an expert in the latest trends in music, media, technology, etc., but *you* likely are, so tell me and teach me so that we can, together, begin to critically reflect on and analyze the world around us." Importantly, this rhetorical strategy isn't about dismissing their references or seeing them as trivial, but rather about addressing them as Gen Z and giving them space to point to cultural change and granting their expertise in seeing that change. In Susan's experience, using this approach has had the effect of getting students excited to share their knowledge with her and establishes a collaborative atmosphere. From there, she has found students are often willing to open themselves up to the new theoretical frame and ways of thinking that the course presents. Similarly, when Susan began teaching she tended to not disclose much about herself or use her own life experiences as fodder for teaching and instead tended to take a more triangulated stance vis–a-vis the course material and the students. But, with age, Susan's teaching persona has become more vulnerable and more strategically self-disclosing, such that she now chooses when to highlight her personal connections to the material in ways that attempt to open up student understanding and empathy.

Finally, while we will focus more explicitly on choosing course materials in Chapter 3, there is a way to think about those choices here in the context of intentionally developing and cultivating one's teaching persona. Some questions to consider: How do we position ourselves in relation to our course materials? Do we see course materials as extensions of our own views or understanding of an issue? Do we explicitly distinguish between our own views/understanding and that of various course materials? Do we even reveal our own positions on issues under discussion? Why or why not?

2.5   Crafting a Classroom Environment

Crafting a classroom environment that is conducive to student learning can be seen as an extension of one's teacherly persona, in that instructors help create a positive classroom environment by modeling the type of behavior that they expect from students. Beyond this, we encourage instructors to give some thought to crafting their classroom environment, and more specifically, to do so at both a relatively abstract big-picture level, as well as in a very concrete sense, at the level of course policy and practice.

It's worth spending some time thinking about how we envision students and how to anticipate and acknowledge that some resistance is almost always going to be a feature of teaching introductory courses that focus on social justice. Given that, how might we think about our role as instructors and the mindset with which we enter the classroom? And how is that mindset shaped by our identities vis–a-vis our students' identities?

In "Unleashing the Demons of History: White Resistance in the U.S. Latino Studies Classroom," Susan Sanchez-Casal writes about the development and evolution of her pedagogy in the face of persistent and predictable resistance from white students. She reflects on the temptations[5] of what she terms "soap-box pedagogy," which she characterizes as "deliver[ing] a righteous lecture about the blindness of white privilege," (2002, p. 73) and "filibuster[ing] my students out of their ways of seeing the world" (2002, p. 74). AnaLouise Keating describes resistance in the Intro class similarly, stating that most students "don't want to learn about social justice; they believe feminism is 'old school' because, after all, women are now equal with men, racism is a thing of the past, and economic disparities are caused by an individual's laziness and can be solved through hard work" (Keating

---

[5]More specifically, Sanchez-Casal acknowledges that she sometimes "resorts to soapbox pedagogy" out of "a sense of self-defense. Out of a desire to survive, to preserve integrity, and to remain whole" (p. 75).

2016, p. 17). Rather than soap-box pedagogy, Keating uses the term "oppositional pedagogical frameworks" to describe the dynamic that she found herself drawn into, which "employ dichotomous either/or epistemologies and generate us-against-them dynamics that pit one person, one group, or one 'Truth' against another" (Keating p. 24). Both Sanchez-Casal and Keating acknowledge how and why instructors (including themselves) often get drawn into this dynamic, even as they argue that this type of pedagogy is ultimately counterproductive, resulting in students' resistance becoming more deeply entrenched, either through protracted argumentativeness or alternately, shutting down and withdrawing completely. As Keating notes, "In such situations, it's much more difficult to even partially achieve progressive, social-justice goals" (p. 25). Sanchez-Casal also grapples with the possibility that soap-box pedagogy not only risks "losing" resistant white students, but also does no favors to students of color, who can find soap-box diatribes "embarrassing and disorienting, as it tends to put Latino/a students even deeper into the hot-seat that they already occupy in the class. Students of color who struggle to find safe and sustaining spaces within the racist structure of a residential private white college may find it counterproductive to line up with the preachy Latina teacher and against the powerful community of white students who feel 'attacked'" (p. 74).

Sanchez-Casal and Keating's characterizations of student resistance in courses with social justice content likely sound familiar. While we have certainly experienced the kind of resistance described by both Sanchez-Casal and Keating, there are additional (perhaps related) dynamics that we as frequently, if not more frequently, experience, and lots of kinds of students beyond what we would call resistant students, including students who aren't really resistant, but nonetheless struggle to grasp the material intellectually, students who read more as apathetic, or just disengaged, and students whose prior learning experiences have not prepared them for the content or pedagogy of a WGS class. One challenge is to not let the resistant students completely determine your approach—how to acknowledge and anticipate them, but not lump everyone into that category. And more broadly, how can we cast a net wide enough, in terms of the classroom environment, to maximize our chances of reaching as many of these categories of students as possible?

Having recognized the limitations of the oppositional soapbox, both Sanchez-Casal and Keating strive for a new approach to pedagogy. Sanchez-Casal uses the term "pedagogical wholeness" and writes of her efforts to remain "open" in the classroom; she also focuses on her quest to carve out an in-between space, "between my authority, knowledge, and desire for students to engage course material openly and willingly and students' desire to maintain and defend their ideological positions" (p. 74). This in-between space, as she sees it, is a place for "organizing a progression of concrete steps that facilitate the possibility of collectively refining and transforming knowledges" (p. 74). Keating also emphasizes openness in her pedagogy; she writes, "I remain open to students' views, while establishing a framework for the course that requires them to analyze their views in dialogue with the required readings. By so doing, I model an attitude of respectful open-mindedness and encourage students to adopt a similar approach" (p. 18). In Chapter 3, we will focus on how to anticipate and respond to specific manifestations of student resistance in the classroom, but our aim here is to inspire reflection about the ethos that instructors bring to the classroom, the big-picture approach to teaching that sets the stage for and animates our policies and practices. While it may be impossible to completely eliminate oppositional, soapbox moments from our teaching, we find much to recommend in what Sanchez-Casal calls pedagogical wholeness and Keating calls pedagogies of invitation. Our discussion of these frameworks is not meant to suggest that these are the only or the correct pedagogical styles, though we find much in them to recommend; rather, our hope is that this discussion will prompt instructors, whether seasoned or relatively inexperienced, to reflect on their own pedagogical values and ethos.

2.6   Course Policies and Classroom Climate

The next move is to consider what your pedagogical values and ethos look like in practice, whether that's a pedagogy of wholeness, invitation, or something else. What kinds of classroom policies are in line with these types of pedagogies? And how are classroom policies translated into concrete practices? For example, do you want to have a written policy (or set of ground rules) in the syllabus regarding classroom behaviors? Would you like to ask students to collaborate with you in creating those ground rules during the first week of classes?

In the past two decades, there has been a slow shift away from the idea that classrooms can/should be "safe spaces." Numerous critiques of the concept have come from instructors who experienced its limitations in their classroom teaching. As Jeannie Ludlow writes, "The problem with 'safety' in the feminist classroom is that it is often proclaimed from a position of innocence regarding the ways cultural spaces are inflected by power and privilege" (2004, p. 4). Drawing on bell hooks' analysis in *Talking Back,* Ludlow asserts that "to the extent, then, that 'safety' is a privilege and a safe space is a privileged space, a safe space classroom is counter to the goals of feminist pedagogy" (p. 5).

As the model of classroom safe spaces has been critiqued, it has been replaced with alternatives, including what Ludlow calls "contested spaces" and what Brian Arao and Kristi Clemens call "brave spaces." Ludlow writes,

> By contested space, I mean a space that is not necessarily defined by conflict, but which includes room for conflict. "Contest" comes from the Latin contestari, which is comprised of con, which means together, and testari, which means to bear witness or to testify. This term, often used to denote "dispute" or "compete," also means to affirm another's witnessing, to testify together. This multi-layered definition provides a more appropriate map for the feminist classroom than "safety". (p. 6)

She uses a Student Bill of Rights and Responsibilities, and identifies six elements that characterize her classroom. "In my experience, the move from the ideology of the "safe space" classroom, with its closed narratives and abdication of power, to the ideology of the contested space classroom, with its open possibilities and overt analysis of power, has provided students (and me) with a conceptual space from which to examine and understand the operations of privilege, oppression, and culture from a locational feminist perspective" (p. 7).

Arao and Clemens see their shift in terminology as "emphasiz[ing] the need for courage rather than the illusion of safety" (2013, p. 141), and go on to discuss how they facilitate conversations around that shift at the beginning of their social justice workshops, asking participants for their thoughts about why they are using the language of bravery rather than safety and what the effects of that linguistic shift might be. Arao and Clemens' change in terminology shifts focus away from the space and onto the people in the space—the "brave" part of brave space is a reference to what is being asked of the people present in the space.

They also focus on the importance and creation of ground rules, helpfully pointing out the importance of making sure that the assumptions embedded in "safe space" discourse don't make a re-entry through the ground rules, especially when an instructor solicits input from students in creating them. While the "brave space" approach was designed for use in social justice workshops, it can also be productively applied to classroom discussions in Intro to WGS classes. However, as Lynn Verduszko-Baker points out, "importing the 'brave space' framework into a semester-long course taken for academic credit requires that instructors be attentive to the differential power dynamics of the classroom to ensure that marginalized students are not negatively impacted and to ensure that instructors themselves are not immune from being 'called in' when necessary" (2018).

In the classroom space, one area that can be highly charged is language usage. Students who feel like they are new to much of the terminology of the course are often afraid of "offending" someone or saying the "wrong" thing. Students who are more resistant to being in a women's and gender studies class may even intentionally not use the terminology of the course as a way to push back against perceived liberal bias. Other students come into the course with a vernacular understanding of a term like "privilege" and that may impede their ability to learn how that term is used in the field of gender studies. And other students will come into the course already fluent (or perceiving themselves to be fluent) in course concepts and terminology; these students may be impatient about an instructor taking class time to clarify these terms, or, more problematically, these students may be quick to judge or correct other students who are fumbling with new language on their learning journey. How does a skilled instructor navigate this terrain in a way that facilitates every student's learning? How can an instructor establish the classroom as a learning space where all students feel safe to stumble as they learn but also space where students from marginalized groups are not cringing and suffering as some students work to acquire a new language? We offer questions without answers here because there is no one right way to approach these issues, though we hope we have offered some starting points for thinking them through in relation to your teacherly persona, as well as classroom policies and practices.

Questions about course policy can also be connected back to the earlier discussion about assigning appropriate weight to particular activities and assignments as a way of conveying their centrality to the course learning objectives. If you value a certain kind (quality) of participation and have crafted a process-related learning outcome, how might you build it into your assessment? Relatedly, do you want to build in a requirement for active participation? If so, what will you count as active participation? Speaking during large-group discussion? Small-group discussion? Posting to a discussion board online? And how might the decision of whether to assess and assign a grade to participation shape the classroom dynamics? The COVID-19 pandemic has drawn attention to the ways that rigid and punitive submission, late work, or attendance policies disproportionately harm marginalized students. This has always been true, but the intensified and more ubiquitous challenges of pandemic learning have made this more visible to a wider range of classrooms, disciplines, and instructors.

2.7   Key Themes and Crafting Your Course

In this last part of this chapter, we look at examples from students' writing to illustrate some of the key ideas and arguments we've made here. One of our intentions is to explicitly show how students who participated in our research engaged with material and grappled with course outcomes. Looking at students' writing in the context of thinking about students' learning outcomes can bring a much-needed specificity or concreteness to our considerations. More specifically, doing so can provide an important reminder of how much and what kind of learning is possible or achievable vis-a-vis the learning outcomes. Overall, we feel strongly that the students' learning outcomes we create and attach to the Intro course should be rooted in the reality of the students that we teach. In this final section, we also consider how the classroom environment we create through our teacherly persona and classroom policies might manifest in our students' written work.

Note: the assignments we refer to throughout this section can be found in Chapter 5; reading the assignments provides additional context for our discussion here.

2.8   Principles for Crafting Your Course: Divergent Entry Points

The relationship between the theme of students' divergent entry points and learning outcomes requires consideration because more often than not, any given section of Intro contains students who are starting from very different places in their learning about and their experiences with social justice efforts, as well as with the academic foundations of the field. This might manifest in different ways. For example, some students may bring with them very limited exposure to the topics or issues, have no previous experience discussing questions of race, gender, class, privilege, or oppression, and may potentially have ideological commitments that require a significant rethinking in order to even engage with the course material. Other students have a significant exposure to some of the social media, online communities, or other digital resources that are available to introduce them to questions about social justice, but may be unfamiliar with engaging in discussions about the topics in an academic or scholarly way. Still other student groups bring with them a significant personal experience with discrimination, trauma, and navigation of oppressive systems, and this provides them with a different lens on the course material. As with most curriculum design, then, you will want to think about how you are accounting for this variation, particularly when it comes to some of the feminist process skills or habits of mind outcomes outlined above—what does achieving those learning outcomes look like at a foundational level, such that you can be satisfied the student is leaving the course with that set of skills or dispositions? What about students who begin the course at that level—might you consider using a different scale of assessment, or a layered and differentiated curriculum that accounts for this level of variation?

Two student case studies illustrate how students' divergent entry points can shape the level of growth they demonstrate—and subsequently require instructors to consider framing learning outcomes that account for this variation in starting and end points. Theresa and Agnes were two students in our research who made strong progress toward the learning goals for the course, and whose prior exposure shaped the level of deep learning they achieved. Theresa, by her own admission, came into the course without much prior knowledge; at the end of the semester, she reflected on the fact that at the outset of the course, "I was used to how aspects were in life, therefore making me not want or feel the need to question the way society portrays things." However, by the concluding reflective essay assignment, she showed an emerging ability to apply the concepts of privilege, oppression, and intersectionality, writing:

> Personally, when having discussions with other classmates about the rich kid and poor kid graph and text, I felt I was shocked. As a child, I was often told that as long as I put my mind towards something, I can achieve and make it anywhere I want. However, although in some cases this may be true, it can be very difficult to actually achieve what I want due to my economic status. What I learned throughout this included the idea that not everything is as it seems. By this, I mean that just because a person works hard at what they do, such as getting their education, doesn't necessarily mean that the person will get where they want to be in life due to oppression.

Dispositionally, she also reported in her final writing for the course that she was taking "baby steps" and acknowledged that "the concept of praxis is a bit scary because it requires going against the status quo: Saying to myself, 'it's okay to feel differently about a subject matter than others do' is a scary thought. Possibly going against others seems terrifying, however, in matters (such as birth control) that pertain a great deal to me personally helps me to move forward and gather the courage to stand up more so for what I believe in." The changes shown by Teresa in her ability to (a) grasp and apply new content; (b) situate her own identity and self-concept within the new material; and (c) metacognitively assess her own learning shows tremendous growth. As with any discipline, of course, instructors need to determine what the "end of course" benchmarks are; for WGS courses, we suggest that learning outcomes need to be flexible and scaled to acknowledge the novelty of much of the course content to most college students and the range of backgrounds they bring with them to the classroom.

Another student participant, Agnes, is representative of the students who bring quite a lot of prior learning with them, either because of life experiences, formal academic study, or independent learning. Agnes, for example, began the course quite capable of recognizing her own and others' identities that influenced their positionality. Interestingly, though Agnes' actual treatment of each of the assessment responses is relatively brief, she concisely and incisively gets at the key issues in the scenarios. For example, in Skills Assessment 2, Agnes analyzes a video of a police stop, quickly identifying how systems of privilege and oppression are manifested in the encounter:

> We will first look at the man who is being oppressed by racism, classism, and ableism. This is clear when the police women states she stopped the man because he had multiple bags and was walking suspiciously. The man is later revealed to be someone who is disabled, and is carrying multiple bags for work. We then look at Jody who is a white women, English speaking, able-bodied, and educated (attorney). Jody is able to use her privilege to speak to the responding officer in the police car without being harassed, and get the man who was stopped to be let go.

Agnes' reflective essay also reports that she had significant prior knowledge, when she writes "To begin, coming into this class I knew a lot about the topic of Women and Gender Studies, yet I was able to still learn more about what I can do to combat inequalities faced within each threshold." Agnes demonstrates a grasp of all of the threshold concepts, including praxis, where she applies her learning retroactively to a prior work situation:

> One way that I can advocate for a transgender individual is to support the creation of gender neutral bathrooms. This is something that I have done back in my hometown at the place that I work, Doller[6] General. We had two identical bathrooms (male/female), one day the female bathroom was being used so a little girl refused to take the male bathroom key. Due to this I was yelled at by the father, I explained to him the situation and he took the key. After they left I came up with a solution inspired by the gender neutral bathrooms here on campus to just give the bathrooms a color that can't be gendered. So

---

[6]Throughout this book, student writing is presented as written.

that the two bathrooms can be gender neutral to avoid future problems with customers as well as being more inclusive to non-binary/transgender individual. The management loved the idea and let us do it, to my knowledge these bathrooms are still gender neutral, this summer when I go back I will attempt to see if I can get that done with other Doller Generals.

Agnes not only demonstrates her understanding of the social construction of gender, privilege, and oppression, including the structural dimensions of oppression, but also accurately identifies how to put that knowledge to use as a form of feminist praxis.

2.9 Principles for Crafting Your Course and Macro-Thinking

A key challenge for students regardless of their entry point into the course material is developing what we described in Chapter 1 as macro-level thinking. That is, it can be difficult for students to link individual experience or the specifics of a given issue with larger structures and systems that serve to shape or construct those experiences and issues. One of the critical distinctions between students who are at a beginning or developing level of understanding of WGS concepts and those who are more advanced is the ability to approach topics from a macro-level perspective. In our research into student learning, we came to see this as a major dividing line, and more often than not, it was a stark division between the students who clearly demonstrated that they had acquired this perspective and those who clearly demonstrated that they had not. Our participating students Mara and Elsa illustrate this issue. We contrast the different progress these students made as a way of inviting readers to think about how to establish learning outcomes that account for the degree to which students can move their thinking from the individual to structural level, a challenge that faces all instructors of socially-engaged disciplines.

Mara made some progress in her work to understand structural contexts for each of the threshold concepts, but her intellectual (and perhaps emotional) attachment to essentialist understandings of sex and gender made it challenging to move past a binary and individualized understanding of the material. For example, in her first skills assessment, in which students are asked to interpret an image of an ambiguously gendered individual standing in front of two gendered restroom doors using the threshold concept of the social construction of gender, Mara immediately assigned a masculine pronoun and gender to the image of the person confronted with a binary bathroom choice, writing:

> In this image, a boy is deciding which public bathroom to use, knowing that if he chooses the girls bathroom he will get yelled at for being a boy in the girl's room, but if he goes in the boy's bathroom he knows he will get beat up by bullies. He clearly knows he will be more comfortable in the girl's bathroom, as his head looks as though it is turned towards the girl's bathroom, but is having a moral dilemma in dealing with either aggressive male bullies or social judgement from his female classmates, as his gender identity seems to be more feminine instead of the "typical" or "wanted" masculine boy.

Unlike many other students, Mara's analysis focuses solely on the person in the image as an individual navigating interpersonal conflict. Her use of quotation marks around the words "typical" and "wanted" suggests that she understands the constructedness of gender, and implies that she is aware of societal-level gender norms, but that's as close as she gets here to offering a structural analysis. Elsa, by contrast, opens her analysis with the following assertion: "this picture demonstrates a possible struggle that transgender, intersex, and non-binary people may have when deciding what bathroom to use inside of a highly gendered and cisgendered system." She goes on to offer a detailed and nuanced analysis of the image that focuses on what she terms "bathroom politics" and "bathroom policy," phrases that signal a macro-level perspective, in addition and in relation to what she calls the "lived reality of transgender, non-binary, and intersex individuals who have had experiences with the bathroom dilemma." At the level of course planning and pedagogy, this issue—an important part of the cognitive and disciplinary work that takes place in the intro course—requires not just recognition and anticipation but also careful design work that can help students navigate this difficult terrain. Determining these benchmarks in socially-engaged fields of study is a necessary challenge to account for in your course planning.

2.10 Principles for Crafting Your Course and Affective Learning

As we discuss throughout the book, affective learning can play a big part in the WGS learning experience. Here we offer a few examples from student work that illustrate affective dimensions of students' learning. The reflective essays that our students wrote at the end of the semester were one place where dispositional learning was often visible. Kerri, for example, wrote about perspective-taking, noting "I have a few people in my life that identify as transgender, the different videos and readings we did encouraged me to see life from their point of view and see issues that they are constantly exposed to." Other students engaged in perspective-taking in their skills assessments. Mel, who identified as a cisgender woman, included the following in her discussion of transphobia: "The way in which I put this into perspective is that of thinking about another individual saying/calling me something I am not. If someone referred to me as a male, I can guarantee I would quickly become angry, as I am sure others would as well. So when I flip it back and look at how transgender or gender non-binary individuals must feel when people do not follow their pronouns I am able to sympathize." We should note that we didn't always have a learning outcome focused on dispositional learning, but after beginning to notice the frequency with which we came across textual moments like these, which indicated that, for many students, empathy and perspective-taking were mechanisms that enabled their acquisition of content-based learning outcomes, we became intentional and explicit about our efforts to cultivate these habits of mind.

2.11 Principles for Crafting Your Course and New Language

As with most fields of study, acquiring new vocabulary and specialized terminology is a key part of the learning that students do, and this vocabulary and terminology will almost certainly appear throughout the learning outcomes you craft for your course. In addition, we suggest giving some thought to how students' acquisition of a new language might play out during class, and how you might take this into account when developing your teacherly persona and creating policies for your course.

Throughout our study, students who were new to the discipline would "misuse" language—for example, using "transgenders" (sic) as a noun to refer to trans people, or using the phrase "colored people" (sic) interchangeably with "people of color." For some of the students in our study, these were new concepts, particularly given our then institution's location in a northern Midwestern state, in a small city where many students came from predominantly white communities of the state. Our observation has been that when an instructor models generosity and invites metacognition about acquiring a new language, students then tend to reflect that back—some even then take that approach with others outside of the classroom. For example, a student named Anna noted:

Right now in college, I am very involved with Cru on campus, which is a non-denominational Christian group. Being a religious organization, women's and LGBT+ rights is a tricky topic because everyone has different views. I have not brought it up a lot but I always try to correct people if they are using the wrong terminology just so they can be aware and not say something harmful without understanding what they are saying.

Though it may be difficult for some students who are coming to the WGS class with a broader set of perspectives and deeper familiarity with disciplinary vocabulary, we find it important to take an instructive approach that assumes goodwill and a willingness to learn on the part of students for whom WGS is a very new field. Having said that, we also believe it is important to model "calling in" students who use outdated, inappropriate, or (intentionally or unintentionally) offensive language.

We hope that the material in this chapter has both convinced you of the importance of starting course planning by thinking about course learning goals and outcomes, and given you some ideas for what sorts of goals and outcomes make sense for your introductory courses. As a part of this work, we also emphasize the importance of your approach to the course, and have provided some food for thought as you consider your teacherly persona and ethos. As you move on to consider course materials and pedagogical activities, please keep these factors in mind, perhaps thinking about these as puzzle pieces that fit together to form the whole of your course.

Works Cited

American Association of College and Universities. VALUE rubrics. https://www. aacu.org/value-rubrics. Accessed 17 January 2021.

Arao, Brian, and Kristi Clemons. 2013. From safe spaces to brave spaces: A new way to frame dialogue around diversity and social justice. In *The Art of Effective Facilitation*, ed. Lisa Landreman, 135–150. Sterling, VA: Stylus Press.

Bartlett, Lesley Erin. 2018. Performing critical generosity in the feminist classroom. *Feminist Teacher* 28: 91–104.

Berger, Michelle Tracy, and Cheryl Radeloff. 2015. *Transforming scholarship: Why women's and gender studies students are changing themselves and the world*, 2nd ed. New York: Routledge.

Berthoff, Ann. 1990. *The sense of learning*. Portsmouth, NH: Heinemann.

Carreiro, Joshua L., and Brian Kapitulik. 2010. Budgets, board games, and make believe: The challenge of teaching social class inequality with non-traditional students. *The American Sociologist* 41: 232–248.

Chakravarty, Debjani. Strata and strategies of teaching about the global "other" using critical feminist pedagogical praxis. *Teaching and Learning Inquiry* 7: 90–105.

Chick, Nancy, and Holly Hassel. 2009. 'Don't hate me because I'm virtual': Feminist pedagogy in the online classroom. *Feminist Teacher* 19: 195–215.

Davis, Dawn Rae. 2010. Unmirroring pedagogies: Teaching with intersectional and transnational methods in the women and gender studies classroom. *Feminist Formations* 22: 136–162.

Hassel, Holly, and Christie Launius. 2017. Crossing the threshold in introductory women's and gender studies courses: An assessment of student learning. *Teaching and Learning Inquiry* 5 (2): 30–46. September.

Hassel, Holly, Amy Reddinger, and Jessica van Slooten. 2011. Surfacing the structures of patriarchy: Teaching and learning threshold concepts in women's studies. *International Journal for the Scholarship of Teaching and Learning* 5. https://digitalcommons.georgiasouthern.edu/ij-sotl/vol5/iss2/18/. Accessed 17 January 2021.

Keating, AnaLouise. 2016. Post-oppositional pedagogies. *Transformations* 26: 24–26.

Kesselman, Amy Vita, Lily D. Kesselman, and Nancy Schneidewind McNair. 2003. *Women: Images and realities, a multicultural anthology*. New York City: McGraw-Hill.

Lang, James M. 2007. Crafting a teaching persona. *Chronicle of Higher Education*, February 6. https://www.chronicle.com/article/Crafting-a-Teaching-Persona/46671. Accessed 17 January 2021.

Lewis, Mel Michelle. 2011. Body of knowledge: Black queer feminist pedagogy, praxis, and embodied text. *Journal of Lesbian Studies* 15: 49–57.

Ludlow, Jeannie. 2004. From safe space to contested space in the feminist classroom. *Transformations* 15.

Sanchez-Casal, Susan. 2002. Unleashing the demons of history: White resistance in the U.S. Latino studies classroom. In *Twenty-First-Century Feminist Classrooms: Pedagogies of Identity and Difference*, ed. Amie A. Macdonald and Susan Sanchez-Casal, 59–86. New York: Palgrave Macmillan.

Scanlon, Jennifer. 1996. Empathy education: Teaching about women and poverty in the introductory women's studies classroom. *Radical Teacher* 48: 7–10.

Schneidewind, Nancy. 1987. Teaching feminist process. *Women's Studies Quarterly* 15: 15–31. *JSTOR*. www.jstor.org/stable/40003433.

Verduzco-Baker, Lynn. 2018. Modified brave spaces: Calling in brave instructors. *Sociology of Race and Ethnicity* 4: 585–592.

Wiggins, Grant, and Jay McTighe. 1998. Backward design. *Understanding by Design*, 13–34. ACSD: Alexandria, VA.

3

Creating Effective Classrooms: Curriculum, Pedagogy and Course Materials

As is suggested by the order of the chapters in this book, it is our belief that course design should flow from thoughtful reflection about the learning goals and objectives chosen for the course and the kind of classroom environment that you want to create. From there, choices can be made about the course materials and pedagogical activities that best support the student learning that you'd like to facilitate in the course, as opposed to starting from and building one's course around the textbook or other course materials. When discussing course design and planning, Land et al. (2005) write about creating a "*framework of engagement*" that "might enable students to experience and gain understandings of the ways of thinking and practising (WTP) that are expected of practitioners within a given community of practice." In other words, having envisioned learning goals for the students in your introductory course, you can now turn to the forms of engagement that best support that learning.

In their introduction to the volume, *Teaching Introduction to Women's Studies: Expectations and Strategies*, Winkler and DiPalma cite Musil's finding that course content, rather than pedagogy, played the biggest role in "students' ability to make connections between course themes and their own lives" (1999, p. 8). Winkler and DiPalma see the combination of course content, along with "student and teacher expectations" and "feminist teaching/learning practices" as key to this outcome. With course outcomes in mind, then, the focus in this chapter is on helping readers do the work of building a learning experience that moves students through and toward those

© The Author(s), under exclusive license to Springer Nature
Switzerland AG 2021
H. Hassel et al., *A Guide to Teaching Introductory Women's and Gender Studies*,
https://doi.org/10.1007/978-3-030-71785-8_3

outcomes, which rests on choices of materials—readings, videos, discussions, lectures—and activities that will invite students into the field and help them achieve the course learning outcomes.

3.1   Choosing Course Materials

As we discussed in Chapter 1, instructors often have divergent approaches to teaching Intro that are strongly rooted in what they believe is the fundamental purpose of the course and/or the specific institutional requirements or mandates. We begin here by characterizing some of these approaches, derived from our program materials, conversations with colleagues, and our own reading and research in online and published materials. Starting with this big-picture view of the introductory course provides a lead-in to thinking more specifically about choices of course materials as well as the rationale behind those choices.

For some instructors, the intro course functions as an introduction to feminist theory, with most of the assigned readings being work written by key feminist thinkers; some versions of this approach focus on change and developments over time, and thus include historical as well as contemporary texts, while others primarily focus on contemporary thinkers and texts. Within this approach to Intro, an instructor might organize the course around certain themes (bodies, work, etc.) and assign students to read intersectional feminist and queer theorizing within these themes. Other instructors might proceed roughly chronologically, contextualizing the tensions within and among feminisms in the past and up to the present. This approach certainly has its advantages, because it allows students to gain a better appreciation for the diversity of feminist theorizing and a historical appreciation of both the changes and continuity over time. The disadvantage of this approach really depends on the student population of the Intro course and the type of institution that the course is taught at. Some students are more prepared than others to grapple with primary sources by diverse authors from different times and places.

Another common approach to teaching Intro is more of a topics-based, coverage approach. This approach tends to lean more into a sociological framework organized around specific societal institutions/sites of privilege, oppression, and resistance. A number of Intro to WGS textbooks are designed using this approach, usually with the first chapter(s) providing a brief historical overview of feminisms. Courses that have this approach might be structured around Taylor, Whittier, and Rupp's textbook, *Feminist Frontiers* (2019), or Shaw and Lee's *Gendered Voices, Feminist Visions* (2019), for example. Advantages of this approach include giving students exposure to a wide variety of topics relevant to the interdisciplinary field of WGS. A limitation might be that it is more challenging for students to see a "throughline" across multiple topics that creates a disciplinary foundation.

Some courses take what we call a "ripped from the headlines" approach; this approach to the introductory course brings forward issues, texts, and phenomena that are currently in the news. The emphasis in this version of the course is on pressing and immediate intersectional social justice issues that are presumably relevant and interesting to the students enrolled. This approach has the advantage of being able to easily demonstrate the continued relevance of the field, and instructors can make the case that the analytical tools that are the hallmarks of the field can help students make sense of these issues and knowledgeably enter into conversation about them. Disadvantages of this approach might be that a focus on very current issues can crowd out treatment of historical or foundational readings and topics that might be considered essential for an introduction to the field.

There are a range of views about whether and how historical inquiry and historical documents should be incorporated into the introductory course. One line of thinking is that it is important for the introductory course to present students with an introduction to the history of feminist thought and activism. Catherine Orr and Ann Braithwaite explicitly reject this approach in their textbook/reader *Everyday Women's and Gender Studies*, stating their intention to "not produce a dominant narrative about WGS origins and objects of analysis born of a singular history that privileges a singular identity category" (2016, p. xv). Some students come into the Intro course expecting it to be a history class because they imagine that gender inequality is a thing of the past, and therefore the focus of a WGS is to study that past inequality. For these students, the inclusion of course materials about the history of feminist thought and activism has the potential to reinforce that understanding.

A different perspective comes from Ilya Parkins, in her review of three Canadian introductory readers. Parkins decries the relative paucity of historical materials; though she acknowledges that "the presentist and future orientation of GWS and especially the Intro course is understandable" (2016, p. 70), she nonetheless argues that "if we want the students we meet in introductory courses to be able to effectively understand difference–arguably the most important broad concept in WGS–then learning about both the historical construction of differences and how feminists have historically engaged with those differences should be a central task" in the course (p. 70). She suggests that facilitating the acquisition of "historical literacy" is an important aim of the introductory course.

Yet another variation on whether and how to incorporate historical inquiry and historical documents into the Intro course comes from Sri Craven, whose "Intersectionality and Identity: Critical Considerations in Teaching Introduction to Women's and Gender Studies" outlines and discusses how she structures her course. While she assigns course materials that are both contemporary and accessible at the introductory level, she spends significant time in class providing what she calls "orienting information" that historicizes the course materials and "capture[s] the broad swath of ideas within which to locate the specific concepts presented by the week's texts" (2019, p. 208). While Craven formally builds this orienting information into the course structure, others take a more informal approach, responding to students' questions about how and why contemporary issues came to be as they organically arise in discussion. For instance, when discussing stereotypes about feminism and feminists, students often inquire where those stereotypes originated. Susan often shows one of many anti-suffrage cartoons from the 1910s that depict suffragists as angry ugly man-haters as a way of quickly demonstrating that these stereotypes were there from the beginning of the use of the word "feminism." Whatever your selected approach, an "outcomes first" architecture can be used to structure the course.

3.2   Considering Textbooks and Readers

Because of the wide range of approaches available to new instructors, we offer here a consideration of some logistical issues to take into consideration when approaching the topic of choosing course materials for the Intro course. Not all instructors have the leeway to choose their primary course materials, perhaps because the choice is made at the departmental level, and all instructors are required to use the same text(s), or perhaps because they have been assigned to teach the course late, after a course text has already been chosen, ordered, and stocked at the campus bookstore. Teaching assistants and part-time instructors are most likely to find themselves in these situations, and thus have to personalize and tailor their course within the parameters of an externally-imposed constraint.

For instructors who have multiple course preps and/or otherwise have major constraints on their time, it is often more convenient to choose from among the many available textbooks and readers that are on the market at a variety of price points. This option can both be a time-saving alternative to the laborious task of individually choosing and curating one's own course readings, clips, films, etc. from scratch, and it can also provide a ready-made structure for the course, which can be especially helpful to instructors teaching the course for the first time.

There is a flip side to this convenience/time-saving factor, however. When we use them in the introductory classroom, textbooks "bear a heavy weight" because they are "the means by which we hope to hail, engage, seduce, and forge an ongoing relationship with our students" (Parkins 2016, p. 68). What's more, as Catherine Orr has pointed out, textbooks "are designed to pass on particular stories about disciplines. And often those textbooks play an outsized role ... in the stories we tell" (p. 12). When deciding whether to use a textbook, and if so, *which* one to use in the Intro course, it is important to think about what stories it conveys about the field, to paraphrase Orr, and whether the stories it conveys are consistent with your values as an instructor and the learning goals you have crafted for the course.

Intro textbooks and readers, of which there are many, carry with them implicit and/or explicit stories about the field, both through the words of their authors as well as through their references, not to mention through their choices of readings. This is not an argument against choosing to use a textbook and/or reader; instead, our suggestion is to choose intentionally and consciously based on whether the story a particular textbook and/or reader tells about the field is consistent with the one you want to share with students, as well as whether it supports your learning goals for the course. What do you want and need your course materials to provide you and your students?

In 2013, Holly and Christie wrote a review of eighteen texts commonly adopted for use in the introductory course[1]; the list included traditional textbooks, combination textbooks/readers, and a few readers. As of this writing, eight of those eighteen have subsequently been published in a newer edition, and of those, six have been updated more than once. The list of titles reviewed in 2013 represents a snapshot in time; in retrospect, that list is indicative of a field in flux. While there are many reasons why a textbook and/or reader might not be updated with a new edition, one reason is that the field changes in significant enough ways that the content of the book loses relevance to instructors and students in the field. Some of the titles on our 2013 list signaled their connection to earlier iterations of the field through their references to "women's studies," as with the Hunter College Women's Studies Collective's *Women's Realities, Women's Choices: An Introduction to Women's*

---

[1]Available here: https://cms.library.wisc.edu/gwslibrarian/wp-content/uploads/sites/26/2015/05/FC34_1-2_TXTBKReview.pdf.

Studies (2014) and Sapiro's *Women in American Society: An Introduction to Women's Studies* (2003).

Titles that have appeared since the 2013 review reflect the direction of the field toward the inclusion of "gender" and/or "sexuality" in the title, as with Braithwaite and Orr's *Everyday Women's and Gender Studies*, Saraswati et al.'s *Introduction to Women's, Gender, and Sexuality Studies* (2020), Gillis and Jacob's *Introduction to Women's and Gender Studies* (2019) and our own *Threshold Concepts in Women's and Gender Studies: Ways of Seeing, Thinking, and Knowing* (2018). Interestingly, two long-running titles have recently been published in their 7th editions with new titles and a new publisher: Shaw and Lee's *Women's Voices, Feminist Visions* became *Gendered Voices, Feminist Visions*, and Kirk and Okazawa-Rey's *Women's Lives: Multicultural Perspectives* became *Gendered Lives: Intersectional Perspectives* (2019).

Holly and Christie's review was guided by a set of evaluative criteria they generated based on what they found important and valuable when teaching the introductory course. We have adapted those criteria here in the form of a heuristic device intended to help instructors find a text or texts that most closely align with the learning outcomes for their course and their pedagogical values.

If you are interested in adopting one of the many textbooks/readers on the market, here is a set of questions to consider as you weigh which selection(s) make the most sense for you:

1. How important is it to you that the text be explicit and transparent about the research and evidence its claims and assertions are predicated upon? More concretely, how important is it to you that the authors/editors include in-text citations?
2. How much, and what kind of a pedagogical apparatus would you ideally like to see in the text?
3. On a related note, would you like to adopt a text that focuses not only on content but also on the cultivation of skills and habits of mind valued in the field?
4. If you are interested in adopting a reader or combination textbook/reader, how robust do you want/need the introductory framing to be?
5. Is the tone and level of the writing a good fit for the students you'll be teaching?
6. Are the references, readings, and/or examples recent and relevant?
7. How important is it to you that the text you choose includes historical material and/or an historicizing perspective in its framing material?

In response to question 1, for example, Holly and Christie's 2013 review expressed a strong appreciation for textbooks that incorporate both in-text citations and bibliographies that establish the evidence-based nature of the field. Doing so, they argue, "models for students the importance of supporting claims with evidence, and it further reinforces the fact that WGS is an established academic field" (p. 11). We would add that it can provide a starting point for responding to student resistance to concepts and frameworks in the field that run counter to students' received ideas about structural inequalities.

By contrast, Braithwaite and Orr provide a different perspective on this issue in the introduction to *Everyday Women's and Gender Studies*. They discuss their decision *not* to include in-text citations as a "democratizing gesture" and as a "form of translation for students just wading into the challenging terrain of difference and power" (p. xviii). For them, it seemed "less relevant that their textbook cite authors and more important that they learn the critical thinking practices WGS emphasizes" (p. xviii). Instead of in-text citations and explicit references to authors, Braithwaite and Orr provide what they call "Chapter Genealogies" at the end of their text, "where few students are likely to venture" (p. xviii). As an instructor, you will want to think about how and whether you plan to encourage students to use such material in the course of their learning. This is an aspect of course material selection that might be significantly shaped by considerations of the local. If you encounter (or anticipate encountering) a fair number of resistant students, you may be drawn to textbooks/readers that include in-text citations and robust bibliographies; conversely, if that is not typically part of the classroom dynamic at your institution, this consideration will be less important.

The subsequent two questions on pedagogy and embedded resources within a textbook acknowledge that some instructors adopt particular texts in part because they appreciate the inclusion of a robust pedagogical apparatus: key terms provided in bold or italics with a glossary in the back, discussion questions, visuals, writing prompts, learning activities, etc. Other instructors may choose the same text but ignore those elements, while other instructors generate and curate their own collection of pedagogical materials over time rather than relying on ready-made ones. If you are shopping around for a text and care about this element, pay careful attention not only to whether there is a pedagogical apparatus included but also to its quality and kind. Less-experienced instructors might particularly appreciate these elements. On a related note, some textbooks and textbooks/readers offer an instructors' guide in addition to including pedagogical materials in the textbook itself.

Possible responses to question 6, regarding currency and examples, may have specific resonance depending on an instructor's disciplinary and academic background. Susan, for example, makes a case for making the Intro course contemporary, with palpable immediacy and a sense of the current issues of our time. Even some of the recent "classic" readings that dominate Intro syllabi can be updated to reflect ongoing debates. For instance, Anne Fausto-Sterling's "The Five Sexes" is a commonly assigned text for good reason, but it was written in the context of discussions in the 1990s. Scientific research on sex and gender identity has advanced a lot in the subsequent decades. If an instructor wants to assign Fausto-Sterling, why not assign Fausto-Sterling's "Why Sex is Not Binary" op-ed in the *New York Times* from 2018? Not only does that piece have a more up-to-date scientific discussion of sex and gender identity formation, but it also ties this discussion in with the Trump administration's proposed memo defining biological sex as fixed and binary.

For Susan's instructional values, selecting current readings is not just about relevancy, either. In the case of "The Five Sexes," it is also about readings that reflect emerging scientific consensus. The Intro course is frequently a gateway course for general-education requirements, and as such, often draws students from all different majors. Students who come from STEM majors are often skeptical that the Intro course is as "rigorous" or "scientific" in the way that they perceive their major courses to be. Especially with the resurgence of biological determinism in white nationalist and Men's Rights Movement (MRM) discourse, it is important to introduce students to the analytical frameworks and scientific research that will give them the tools to see through the claim that gender studies is fundamentally unscientific. In recent years Susan has assigned Hyde et al., "The Future of Sex and Gender in Psychology: Five Challenges to the Gender Binary" as a supplemental reading for students who are STEM majors and who want to further explore current research into sex/gender. You will want to do similar kinds of thinking about what your academic background offers, how to select a textbook or materials that comports with your values, and what the specific course outcomes and student needs are that can be met with those teacherly choices.

3.3   Beyond Textbooks

In this section, we shift our focus away from textbooks specifically, toward a discussion of choices of course materials more broadly, whether you eschew a textbook altogether, or supplement a text with additional materials. The four main insights that emerged from our SoTL study all have clear relevance to the choices we make about the course material we use in the introductory course.

When choosing written course materials, particularly explicitly academic sources such as textbooks, journal articles, or chapters in edited collections, we recommend giving some thought to the amount and kind of specialized language, whether technical, theoretical, or just disciplinary. This is not an argument against choosing reading material that contains specialized language, but instead is a suggestion about making intentional choices in this regard, given that much of the learning that takes place in the introductory course centers around grappling with a new language for thinking and talking about gender, sexuality, and structural inequality. For example, in our experience, students often express appreciation for textbooks that provide a glossary of terms, or readings that otherwise offer clear definitions of specialized language. Instructors who decide against using a textbook or textbook/reader might want to consider some other mechanism for providing students a reference guide to relevant terms and concepts. For instance, an instructor might engage students in a "muddiest point" exercise at regular intervals throughout the semester.

On a related note, one way to accommodate students' divergent entry points to the introductory course is to choose course materials that offer varying levels of complexity and difficulty on any given topic. Doing so gives those students with little background knowledge a place to start to establish their footing, while also providing a challenge for students building on pre-existing knowledge.

One possibility is to scaffold the sequence of course readings over several class periods, building toward the more complex and/or technical material; a different approach would be to assign multiple texts for a given class period that cover roughly similar ground, but range from broadly accessible to denser/containing more theoretical or technical language. A variation on this is to ask students to read a journalistic summary and discussion of a relevant, peer-reviewed journal article or report, particularly if the summary includes a link to the journal article or report itself. Sociologist Lisa Wade's summary and discussion of psychologist Niobe Way's work on boys' friendships in *Salon* (2013) is a good example of this; Claire Cain Miller's discussion in the *New York Times* of a recent study by sociologist Amy Hsin on the effects of masculine gender norms on boys' academic achievement is another (2019). Both articles provide links to the work that is being discussed; some instructors might stick with having the students read the discussion of the primary source, while others might subsequently ask students to read some or all of the original source to deepen their understanding.

Given the prominent role of the affective realm and of affective learning in the introductory course, we recommend taking this into account when choosing course materials. First-person narratives that invite and encourage students to take the perspective of someone who has directly experienced structural oppression can be useful in this regard; depending on the student, the affective response might be one of resonance and recognition, if they are positioned similarly and/or have experienced something similar, or surprise and shock, if the narrative recounts experiences they have not had, or if it is written by someone positioned significantly different than they are. When choosing research-based material, we recommend including pieces by qualitative researchers who intentionally incorporate the voices of the peoples/communities that are the focus of the research. Beyond written texts, we have found both short-form and longer-form documentaries, as well as StoryCorps segments, Ted Talks, and podcasts to be especially useful for their potential to facilitate affective learning. As instructors, we also make intentional choices about course material that can support students' acquisition of a sociological imagination, support their ability and willingness to see and understand structural dimensions of privilege and oppression, and locate themselves within those structures. Among the types of course material that facilitate this intellectual work are first-person pieces that provide a meta-level narration of and reflection on that process.

3.4   Designing Pedagogical Activities that Flow from Our Values and Facilitate Student Learning

When it comes to decisions about how to use classroom time, after many years of teaching the introductory course, all three of us start from a place of insight gained from trial and error over time. We have spent a lot of time thinking about how and where students tend to get "stuck" in their learning in the Intro course, and what aspects of the course and course material many students struggle with. Relatedly, we have also thought about where we tend to be met with resistance. Much of this reflective thinking has taken place in the context of evaluating student work. We have then taken the insights we have gleaned about student learning in the Intro course and brought them back to our thinking about how to use class time to help students get "unstuck," to overcome their resistance, and/or to help them through those periods of struggle in their learning. In what follows, we will sketch out what we see as some of the most common learning roadblocks (a term Christie and Holly have incorporated into their introductory textbook) and offer suggestions for pedagogical activities that can facilitate students' learning. The four themes from our SoTL project (divergent starting points, new language, macro-level thinking, and affective learning) are woven throughout this section.

As we have previously noted, students can bring their own pre-existing frameworks and understandings of the topic into the classroom with them in ways that can help or hinder their movement toward the course goals and outcomes. In *How Learning Works: 7 Research-Based Principles for Smart Teaching*, Ambrose and colleagues note that students are not blank slates and come to our courses with knowledge that is an "amalgam of facts, concepts, models, perceptions, beliefs, values, and attitudes, some of which are accurate, complete, and appropriate for the context, some of which are inaccurate, insufficient for the learning requirements of the course, or simply inappropriate for the context" (p. 13). In the case of women's and gender studies, students bring a lifetime of classed, gendered, and racialized experiences with them, and the analytical lenses that emerge from those experiences can frequently either enhance or interfere with their ability to engage course materials/concepts/frameworks, depending on a variety of factors, including their relative positioning within structures of privilege and oppression. For example, students operating out of positions of privilege are often unaware of those pre-existing lenses and/or think of them as "common sense."

The research literature on transfer—or the ways that learners bring prior knowledge and skills to use in new situations—is robust. Haskell defines transfer as "...how previous learning influences current and future learning, and how past or current learning is applied or adapted to similar or novel situations" (quoted in Elon 2013). As a kind of analog to misconceptions (in which students might bring a misunderstanding of the topic to women's and gender studies), negative transfer can bring a misunderstanding to the classroom, or apply non-relevant knowledge to the new setting.

What is important to remember as a teacher is that students' self-concepts are powerful and ingrained. The threshold concepts and other new ways of seeing, thinking, and knowing can be tremendously disruptive to students' existing sense of themselves in both positive and negative ways. For some students, they can provide a liberating new set of ideas and terms that speak to their lived reality; for others, such ideas and terms challenge their existing ways of thinking about themselves and the world. In "Racism as a Threshold Concept: Examining Learning in a 'Diversity Requirement' Course," Erin

Winkler notes that this was the case in the course she studied systematically, observing that "If part of a threshold concept is that it is 'troublesome knowledge' that necessitates a paradigm shift…it is likely that this shift may be more difficult for students whose sense of self may potentially be troubled by" it (p. 820). Accounting for this paradigm shift through pedagogical and curricular structuring is an important part of designing our courses.

One final note before we sketch out the learning roadblocks we frequently encounter. For the three of us, identifying these learning roadblocks has been a part of a larger process of cultivating a pedagogy of invitation. As teachers, we have become more and better prepared to respond to them by comparing notes and articulating what learning roadblocks are common for students in WGS. And perhaps more importantly, it has led to a mental shift in our approach to teaching the course. Rather than having an internalized ideal Intro class in our heads, and then feeling like we and/or our students have fallen short of the mark when these sorts of roadblocks inevitably crop up, we have instead reframed them and incorporated them into our pedagogical strategies. As well, naming and sharing these roadblocks with students can help them see that it is not a failure and indeed, not even unusual, for students who are new to this material to struggle. Naming them as common and even normal serves a pedagogical purpose in helping students be okay with grappling with these habits of mind, learning outcomes, and skills of WGS and other socially engaged classrooms, and that such grappling is even necessary for growth.

3.5   Learning Roadblocks

- **Misconceptions about the field**: As previously mentioned, the greater availability of voices and data online and in social media spaces means that students may come in with both greater awareness of but simultaneously greater levels of misinformation about feminist thinking, theory, and activism. It is increasingly likely that students coming into the WGS classroom will have seen a YouTube video that "destroys" the concept of intersectionality, for instance, or a student who has "heard" about a college professor that refuses to call on white men. Instructors need to be able to deftly neutralize the "fake news" that students might introduce into the classroom, while at the same time being generous and empathetic with the students who are understandably misled by these deliberate and ubiquitous misrepresentations. For instance, in a classroom discussion on stereotypes about feminism and the ways that feminists get labelled as "radical," a student once raised her hand and said she had read a story on Facebook about a woman who filed a sexual harassment lawsuit against the man that saved her from drowning and that she thought that some feminists were taking things too far. Christie was so caught off guard that she didn't quite know what to say and the rest of the students then were drawn into this salacious claim. But the "news story" was in fact a satirical anti-feminist meme that was making the rounds on the internet. So, it is crucial for an instructor to model generosity while at the same time maintaining a firm hold on the direction and tone of the classroom discussion.

- **Gender Essentialism**: Certainly for some students and student populations, notions of fixed sexual and gender identities will be the default. This can range from lack of familiarity with non-binary gender identities to beliefs about the inherent and generalizable nature and characteristics of boys and girls, men and women (e.g., "boys will be boys"). The backlash to the increasing visibility of transgender people and the advancement of transgender rights has only increased claims to gender essentialism about the supposed inherent differences between the sexes. Students increasingly enter the WGS classroom wondering about the place of transgender girls and women in sports, for instance, or they will have heard the term Trans-Exclusionary Radical Feminist (TERF) and they will ask about its place in the course. Students from certain religious traditions might come into the course with a belief that their religious faith dictates a complementarian view of gender that affirms different roles and skill sets for men and women.

- **Response v. analysis**: Many students come into the Intro class with a mistaken notion that the course content is "just a bunch of opinions," and that their role in the course is just to respond to the material by providing their own opinion. Relatedly, reaction and a rush to judgment can easily be substitutes for analysis and examination. Students can be tempted to talk in simplistic terms of "good" and "bad" representation, "degrading" versus "positive" images, and use other value-laden terms, perhaps as newcomers to academic language and genres, or out of a mistaken belief that that is what their instructor wants to hear. Frequently, these evaluative judgments are cursory and dismissive and take the place of more in-depth and nuanced analyses.

- **Misreadings**: In some instances, students produce misreadings of course material because they read too quickly or carelessly; we have certainly also taught students whose critical reading skills were not very developed, such that they sometimes struggled to understand key points and arguments in assigned texts. In the context of the introductory WGS course, one particular type of misreading that we have noticed is when a student mistakenly thinks that an author who is describing structural inequality in order to *critique* it is actually perpetuating it. Another type of misreading we have encountered is more clearly rooted in resistance to the course material; in this version, a student might accuse an author of being racist or sexist for documenting and discussing racism or sexism. This rhetorical strategy of claiming that talking about racism is itself racist can also be seen, of course, outside the classroom.

- **Struggles with Macro-Level Thinking**: Many students use their personal experience and direct observation as their basis for understanding social issues, and as the yardstick they use to generate knowledge about the world, which can cause difficulties when they are asked to adopt and develop a sociological imagination in introductory courses. For example, we have encountered many students with an evangelical Christian background who express shock that only 5% of heterosexual people haven't had intercourse before marriage because it differs so vastly from their personal observations. When teaching in states like GA and MS, we have encountered many students, both Black and white, who persist in their assumption that the racial composition of the rest of the United States mirrors that of the South. And finally, all three of us taught for many years in WI, where students widely assumed, based on their personal observations, that sports culture in relation to gender norms works the same across the United States. Especially because personal experience can be brought to bear so powerfully in the WGS classroom, it is important for instructors to discuss the limitations of anecdata and model how to value and assess both personal narratives and social science research.

- **Regression (liminality)**: Over the years, we have frequently seen students perform understanding or use of a particular lens cultivated in the course in one setting, but revert to an old understanding when applied to a new set of data, information, or text. Meyer and Land name a similar principle "liminality," in which learners move back and forth in the substance and accuracy of new understanding, occupying a kind of liminal space in which their new way of thinking is not consistently deployed or applied. For example, In *Teaching about Race and Racism in the College Classroom*, Cyndi Kernahan discusses the importance of accepting that learning is not a linear process. As she writes, "Just when I think everyone is starting to get the concept of institutional racism, for example, someone will make a comment or interpret a course reading in a way that tells me that they do not understand and cannot apply it to new examples" (p. 7). This liminality is, in fact, an essential part of learning: learners grapple with new ideas, perspectives, and information, but it's important to know that this process is accompanied by a struggle to integrate that new understanding with their existing understanding. It also speaks to the importance of giving students multiple and varied opportunities to demonstrate understanding.

- **Struggles with New Language**: There are several ways that struggles with the language of the course might manifest. Students learning about transgender, non-binary, and/or gender non-conforming identities for the first time, for example, may struggle to incorporate gender-neutral pronouns into their vocabulary. The broader learning struggle has to do with their encounter with a non-binary framework for understanding sex and gender, but at the moment that might manifest as a very specific form of linguistic struggle. Students may also struggle to incorporate course concepts into their own thinking, writing, and speech, in ways that result in stilted prose, awkward sentence constructions, or struggles to be coherent. It is important for instructors to anticipate these struggles with new language and also to value them as signs of learning!

- **Affective Dimensions of Learning**: Students don't learn, or don't learn as much, if they are not connected to the instructor. Establishing students' trust in you as an instructor is a key that can help unlock learning, especially in an introductory WGS course (see Baker et al. 2013; Bevilacqua et al. 2019; National Academies 2018). Many students enter the classroom skeptical, anxious, or even scared of the course and by extension the instructor. Questions they might ask themselves: Is this instructor going to be an angry feminist? Will I get reprimanded if I don't say the "right" thing in the "right" way? Glynis Cousin characterizes students like these as "defended learners." On the other hand, students from underrepresented groups might come in with different fears and anxieties, especially on campuses that are Predominantly White Institutions (PWI). Questions they might ask themselves: Will I have to sit uncomfortably in class while other students doubt the existence of privilege and inequality, question my right to exist, or the legitimacy of my identity? Will this instructor intervene when needed? Does this instructor really "get it"? Or do they think they are "woke" in ways that demonstrate that they are not? Navigating this terrain and fostering connection with all students is not easy, but this emotional labor lays a foundation for learning.

3.6 Anticipating and Addressing Learning Roadblocks

The good news is that these are roadblocks that instructors can anticipate and structure class activities and instruction in ways that help surface them, as well as encourage students to move past what can be barriers to thinking with and through more critical perspectives on the material. A Student's ability and willingness to work through the roadblocks to their learning vary widely of course, and is more often than not shaped by what the source of their roadblock(s) is/are, i.e., if they are encountering structural analyses of society for the first time, whether or not they are overtly resistant to the course material, whether their roadblocks are rooted in a lack of awareness of privilege, etc. In this next section, we provide some specific strategies for doing so, as well as highlight three student case studies that offer "snapshots" of progress over the course of a semester.

Misconceptions about the Field: As we have made clear, the greater availability of voices and data online and in social media spaces means that students may come in with both greater awareness of but simultaneously greater levels of misinformation about feminist thinking, theory, and activism. Kernahan cites the work of Lewandowsky on how best to counter misinformation and makes the case that it is important to "repeatedly provide a new, alternative story," i.e., a different framework for seeing, thinking about, and understanding the world (her focus is on systemic racism), and "ignore or at least minimize" the misinformation you're trying to counter (in her example, that's the concept of so-called colorblindness. As she puts it, "According to the research, engaging with misinformation directly inadvertently strengthens peoples' belief in that misinformation" (p. 35). Kernahan here does not suggest that we should literally ignore this misinformation, but instead should not lend it credence by engaging it at length and on the terms that it is presented.

For example, when discussing non-binary individuals, a class conversation that is not structured well can quickly devolve into debates about the existence or legitimacy of non-binary people and their attempts to define their own identities. But, if the instructor frames the discussion deliberately, then the class discussion tends to take a different path. For instance, starting with recent public polling data from the Pew Research Center on generational awareness of non-binary people (35% of Gen Z polled knew someone who uses gender-neutral pronouns) prompts students to discuss how their generation perhaps thinks about identity and inclusion differently than previous generations. The class discussion then becomes more forward-looking—"what are the implications of the shifts that are taking place around us?" rather than a more presentist debate—"how do we feel about these changes right now?"

Essentialism: Explicitly talking with students about gender essentialism as a learning roadblock allows them to examine where and when they've encountered these kinds of claims in their life. This is part of the process of "unlearning" received wisdom or complicating what we are often told is just "common sense." Students are generally receptive to this and see the benefits of a more nuanced view of how biology and culture are both influential when discussing gender identity, gender norms, and gender roles. Especially when instructors introduce some of the surprising and complex ways that human bodies vary, students easily grasp how a reductive essentialism flattens an otherwise richly textured embodied reality. Instructors can also use learning roadblocks as an invitation to practice the kind of analysis that they will need for upcoming assessments. For instance, an instructor can reflect on common student missteps from previous semesters and intentionally craft small group discussions around the kind of analysis that students need to succeed. In this way, there is a productive feedback loop between meaningful assessment (discussed in more depth in Chapter 4) and intentional pedagogy. While students generally quickly grasp why gender essentialism is overly simplistic, many of them might not readily grasp how the process of gender socialization often functions to prop up essentialism by "naturalizing" the gender binary. But, when small group discussion is structured around generating examples of how this works (e.g., body norms around hair), then students can more easily practice the sort of analysis that is a learning outcome for the course and will be needed as evidence for assessment.

Response v. Analysis: We find it helpful to use class time, particularly at the beginning of the semester, to discuss the difference between response and analysis, and to provide and discuss examples of each. We also find it helpful to be very explicit about when we're asking students to respond to a text and when we're asking them to analyze it. To help students navigate new ways of approaching texts and ideas, we recommend practicing a scaffolded approach to each class period or activity, which can include an "I do/We do/You do" staged approach. When applying or using new material, starting by modeling the intellectual moves that you want students to make is succeeded by a collective classroom activity that does the same kind of intellectual work, before asking students to move to independently use that new lens or concept. In Chapter 5, we include an example of an assignment that asks students to write a brief narrative modeled after a StoryCorps segment. This assignment comes after listening to and discussing several of these stories, then workshopping their emerging drafts with peers during class.

Practicing New Language: Given that students often struggle to incorporate discipline-specific concepts and frameworks into their thinking and writing, we believe it is important to structure in opportunities for students to have those struggles and to give them some tools and strategies for navigating that liminal learning space. For example, in the context of a unit on the social construction of gender, we spend some time in class examining sample sentence constructions that clearly convey that gender is socially constructed, and compare them to sentence constructions that convey a belief, through word choice, that gender is innate. For example, we compare a sentence that starts "Men are…" with a sentence that starts "Men are expected to be…" and talk about the different meanings that are conveyed by them.

As discussed in the first part of the chapter, many students appreciate when a textbook or textbook/reader provides a glossary, and that desire for a glossary doesn't go away when an instructor decides to forego the use of a textbook or textbook/reader. One idea for filling this gap is to ask students to generate their own glossary by spending some class time identifying key terms and concepts, individually or in groups. The instructor could create a shared document that logs all of these terms and concepts, and update it continuously throughout the semester. As students encounter new texts that utilize the same terminology, they can revisit and update their definitions, noting differences in how authors define and/or use the terms.

Helping students through the liminal space and supporting transfer: We have found that student learning is enhanced by assignments or tasks that ask them to apply course concepts to their area of academic interest (such as a major, minor, or future career). As a sort of "utility-value intervention" (Harackiewicz et al. 2016), tasks that ask students to connect, for example, course material to areas that they recognize will be part of their future career and coursework can have particularly high-impact benefit. Students in our research project made particularly strong connections to their future careers in social work, psychology, criminal justice and law enforcement, nursing, athletic training, librarianship, and a host of other imagined prospective future contexts, as we will discuss in greater detail in Chapter 4.

Cultivating macro-level perspectives and encouraging analysis: We are pairing these two together as we see connections between these two areas. For some students, offering only opinion-based responses, as opposed to using a response as a starting point for more in-depth analysis, is rooted in a struggle to adopt a sociological imagination. In a classroom context, we might ask students to write a short response to an assigned text and then to engage in dialogue, in small groups, so that they can hear others' responses and begin to consider how those responses are shaped by their identities and experiences. We might also ask students to revisit their initial response at the end of a class period and to spend a few minutes reflecting on whether and how the classroom discussion shaped their thinking.

Attachment to the Known and Cultivating Metacognition: Because students' views on gender, race, class, and other identities are so deeply tied to self-concept, it is important in this course to give students many structured opportunities to do low-stakes writing and reflection in ways that are not necessarily labor-intensive for the instructor (or even graded) but that allow for feedback and metacognition. It is important to structure classroom activities that allow for students to express why they might be struggling with a new concept or framework, but to do so in a way that doesn't derail other students' learning. One example of how to accomplish this is to ask students at the end of each class to write down one question that they had from the day's material and/or discussion. At the beginning of the next class period, the instructor can then pick out a few of these questions to answer and contextualize. This gives the instructor a chance to affirm students' curiosity and sometimes confusion, but also lets the instructor do so in a direct and brief way that doesn't pull the entire class discussion off into a tangent or a misunderstanding. It is also important for instructors to address—head-on—common misconceptions in the women's and gender studies classroom. Some other types of activities that can support this work include:

- Reflective papers that ask students specifically to self-assess their learning and to set goals for future learning.
- Low-stakes writing and journal entries where students can document emerging questions or topics they are struggling with in the course content.
- "Exit tickets," one-minute papers, or other short prompts on notecards at the end of a class (if in a face-to-face class), collected by the instructor and quickly reviewed to identify common issues, questions, or insights that students are grappling with.
- Use of Twitter, blogs, Slack, or other digital spaces where students and the instructor can engage in a written dialogue about the material, which can give students some space and time to think but also participate in an interactive conversation that might be difficult for more introverted, struggling, or generally quiet students to make their voices and insights visible.

The specific learning experiences of students are most helpful to unpack in order to understand how particular pedagogical strategies, content emphasis, and assessment considerations operate.

3.7   Working Through Learning Roadblocks: Case Studies

To close this chapter, we offer three brief case studies of students, with a discussion of what some of the learning roadblocks can look like as students progress through the course. Likewise, we identify pedagogical approaches and emphases that seemed to have particular resonance for these three students.

Structuring opportunities into the course for students to manage and reflect on those affective dimensions of their learning is one important opportunity to help students process, as well as link, the emotional and dispositional parts of their learning with their academic and intellectual growth. **Reflective writing** proved a particularly important component for Joy, a southeast Asian student who made explicit connections between the course material and her own prior experiences. Joy did not have prior experience with women's and gender studies coursework, or with socially engaged curricula, and some areas of critical analysis demanded in the class were extremely challenging for her. She often defaulted to heavy quoting of the textbook, in a way that suggested that she had a hard time articulating course concepts in her own words. More specifically, her skills assessments showed that she struggled to understand intersectionality as it related to trans issues as well as the connections between racist and sexist oppression. However, Joy's end-of-semester reflective essay demonstrated evidence of tremendous growth. The prompt for that assignment asked students to "Describe what you have learned about each of the four threshold concepts, including the relationship between them" and "how you might use that knowledge to engage in your communities to advocate for social justice and create a more equitable world, in ways both big and small." Joy skillfully analyzed her personal experience through the lens of several key course concepts, including horizontal hostility and internalized oppression[2]:

> I felt like I was walking the fine line between being Hmong and being American. I grew up in a predominately white town, so I had a lot of white friends. I

---

[2]Student writing is presented as written.

was referred to as "the asian" and was constantly told I was "the whitest Asian." This caused a lot of internalized oppression, which is defined as "members of marginalized groups come to internalize the dominant group's characterizations of them as lesser and inferior" (94). I internalized the oppression by thinking being Asian wasn't enough, that's why I had to be the "whitest" Asian. I also was always assumed to be smart and very good at math and science because Asians are stereotyped to be good in those subjects. In return, I let them call me "the whitest Asian" just to fit in. I dressed more "white" and acted like I came from the same economic class as my friends. Unintentionally, I looked down on people of my own kind. I found myself beginning to show horizontal hostility, which "happens when a member of a marginalized group identifies with the values of the dominant group" (94). I began to think I was better than my Hmong peers because I had white friends. I cut off all my Hmong friends because I thought opportunities for me would open up for me. My white friends were in sports and in all sorts of extra-curriculars, which in my eyes, was the cool thing to do.

She further identifies privilege and oppression operating through her personal experience:

> I thought if I tried to fit in with my white friends despite me being Hmong, I would be more privileged. In hindsight, I was never going to be as privileged as my white friends because I did not have the same benefits and advantages and power as they would have. I began to realize I would not have been able to go to UW Madison like my friends, not because I wasn't smart enough to get in, but because my parents would not have been able to afford it. I began to see how different their parents treated me because I was Asian, especially by asking me if I was okay with eating pizza rather than stir fry. Although oppression may happen without even knowing it, it happens on an everyday basis. Perhaps people are ignorant to the fact that they may be privileged and the way they act may be oppressive, but being on the other side of privilege is not a great place to be.

Though students had previous opportunities throughout the course that asked them to define and apply these concepts (privilege and oppression in Unit 2, and intersectionality in Unit 3), it was the final *reflective* assignment that allowed Joy a place in the course's formal work to explore the collective concepts around which the course is structured, as well as provide her with a lens through which to describe and analyze her own identity development. As the three of us discussed Joy's written work over the course of the semester, we were reminded of the importance of giving students a wide variety of discussion questions, writing prompts, and classroom activities. In Joy's case, we speculate that the learning roadblocks she experienced in the earlier parts of the semester might have been overcome more readily had we realized how powerful it would be for her to analyze her own experience through the lens of course concepts.

A second case study helps further illustrate some of the learning roadblocks. Miley entered the class with some misconceptions and antipathy toward feminism, reflecting divergent entry points that included not just ideas that were new to her but that she had negative preconceptions about. In her reflective essay, she "talked back" to her initial impressions, writing, "I was under the impression that [the course] was all about feminist stuff and don't get me wrong I'm all for women's rights but I really just believe in treating everyone equally." Her understanding of the course concepts and issues evolved rapidly but also at times unevenly. In her first skills assessment, for example, Miley refers to gender-reveal parties as a "cute new trend" and writes in response to the prompts with reactive rather than analytical language, although with a sometimes humorous voice. For example, she offered a wry assessment of the commercial she was asked to analyze: "When the [voiceover in the] commercial asks should the phone be a racehorse duct-taped to a Scud missile fast, I really don't even know what that means," and later she addressed the social construction of gender by noting: "So from the beginning it is trained for boys to throw some dirt on it and call it a day but for the girls it is okay for you to cry because that is what is expected. I think this is very unhealthy for men, especially young boys. It's mentally destructive." She is a good example of a student who was new to the language of academic analysis, but particular parts of the course material were more accessible to her because of her awareness of the aspects of her own identity that placed her in a marginalized group. In the privilege and oppression assessment, she references her own identity from what she calls a "low middle class family," writing:

> I came from a very low middle class family. Close to poor. Grew up in a small town. What do you think I faced all through school? Being talked to and about differently because I don't have the privilege that others in my class have. Money and the big name. I'm just an average kid working my way through the best I can. The stigma that puts on me is even bigger.

Throughout the writing activities, we saw Miley grappling with moving into macro-thinking while drawing from her own experience of sexism and gendered family expectations. In her second skills assessment, she recounts being made to feel invisible when her grandmother ignores her and speaks only to her boyfriend. She continues,

Like excuse me? I deserve respect too. I may not know everything about cars and fixing things but I'm gonna be a nurse one day. Will I be respected then? To have my own grandmother favor my boyfriend, right in front of me. As if I haven't been apart of her life for 20 years and he's been apart of her life for 5 years. That's the saddest of all oppression I have ever experienced. So why are men privileged when they post naked pictures of women and why are the women talked about in such dirt manner? I'm still waiting for the answer because I do not know. I can't wrap my head around this messed up concept.

The language of academic analysis is clearly not used here, but Miley is making connections between internalized oppression and the social construction of gender, and she is asking questions that are trying to get at macro-level explanations for what are painful and difficult struggles for her as a working-class white woman.

Miley's third skills assessment revealed that she struggled to employ an intersectional analytical lens. In response to the prompt that asked her to analyze a tv clip, she defaulted to using a gendered lens that could not account at all for its blatantly racialized dimensions. She was, however, able to find access to the concept of intersectionality through her interest in career aspiration of nursing. In the prompt that asked her to choose a topic discussed in the course through an intersectional lens, she wrote, "I am using maternal mortality because these were one of my favorite topics with it relating to much of healthcare so I can relate easier." Even here, though, the tentative nature of her understanding was manifested by the fact that her analysis consisted of a series of questions rather than assertions. She writes, "When you put it all together with a lens of intersectionality especially with Jessica's case, would the outcome be differently of someone who was not white?"

Like Joy, the reflective essay assignment allowed Miley to develop and share a metacognitive assessment of her own understanding. In her reflective essay, she observed: "Intersectionality combined gender, race, and culture all into one, so a mixture of all and how they meet or intersect in the middle and all come together. This section was probably the hardest concept for me to grasp." We see Miley demonstrating the key themes of learning over the course of the semester, and some of the common learning roadblocks we described in this chapter. Important interventions both pedagogical and in course design included inviting connections to personal experience and opportunities to reflect on her own identity in relation to the course concepts; invitations to make connections to her career and educational goals were also important in the unit of intersectionality.

The work of a third student, Mara, shows how students encounter and navigate some of these learning roadblocks; we have chosen some quotes from her work that focus on some of the preconceptions she brought into the course, as well as her struggles to adopt a macro-level perspective and analysis. In her reflective essay she writes, "Coming into this course I was very skeptical of what we would do because I knew that a lot of the topics discussed probably would not match my personal political views, however I found that many of the topics seem like things I would be interested in advocating for." Mara was able to make some progress in understanding how her prior disposition is compatible with at least some components of feminist praxis: "Look at me, someone who came into this class knowing virtually nothing about these issues, and now I feel so strongly about so many of them and want to be an advocate for these issues, that if we can mandate education for more people like me, maybe these issues really could be put to rest because more people will be interested in them once they learn about them." Though her understanding remains interpersonal and individual (for example, reflecting the belief that education or awareness rather than structural change to systems is a tool for equity), Mara's case provides an opportunity to reflect on what it looks like for students to work through a learning roadblock.

Like many other students, we observed that Mara was particularly eager to engage with the course material when making connections with her future career as a healthcare worker, though again, these interventions remained on an interpersonal and individual level:

> I have learned a great amount of information that I can relay into my future as a healthcare worker. These topics include Implicit bias training, the definition of an ally and how to be one to others, as well as medical advances such as being trained in mental health in regards to postpartum depression as well as knowing the signs and symptoms of abuse. When used together, I believe that these skills will make me a nurse that people can go to and feel as though they are being heard, cared for fairly, and treated with respect.

Her application of concepts of allyship and implicit bias shows clear progress in her thinking and analysis from the start of the course, even though they remain at a micro and exclusively interpersonal level. We invite readers here to think about strategies for helping students work through what for many of them is an admittedly extremely challenging paradigm shift.

Pedagogical and course design choices are going to vary from course to course, but we hope that by reflecting on the values that you have as an instructor, those necessary adjustments that accompany any new group of students can be rooted in disciplinary best practices that also reflect your individual strengths, background, and instructional goals. Chapter 4 focuses on the reciprocal relationship between selecting course materials, designing learning activities, and assessing students' development of those skills and their grasp of content knowledge.

Works Cited

Ambrose, Susan, et al. 2010. *How learning works: Seven research-based principles for smart teaching*. San Francisco, CA: Jossey-Bass.

Baker, Michael, Jerry Andriessen, and Sanna Jarvela. 2013. *Affective learning together: Social and emotional dimensions of collaborative learning*. New York: Routledge.

Bevilacqua, Dana, et al. 2019. Brain-to-brain synchrony and learning outcomes vary by student-teacher dynamics: Evidence from a rel-world classroom electroen-cephalography study. *Journal of Cognitive Neuroscience* 31: 401–411. https://doi.org/10.1162/jocn_a_01274.

Braithwaite, Ann, and Catherine Orr (eds.). 2016. *Everyday women's and gender studies: Introductory concepts*. Routledge: New York.

Chinn, Sarah, et al. 2014. *Women's realities, women's choices: An introduction to women's studies*. New York: Oxford University Press.

Craven, Sri. 2019. Intersectionality and identity: Critical considerations in teaching introduction to women's and gender studies. *Frontiers* 40: 200–228.

Elon University Center for Engaged Learning. 2013. Elon Statement on Writing Transfer Working Draft. http://www.elon.edu/docs/e-web/academics/teaching/ers/writing_transfer/Elon-Statement-Writing-Transfer.pdf.

Fausto-Sterling, Anne. 2018. Why Sex is Not Binary. *New York Times*, October 25.

Gillis, Melissa, and Andrea Jacobs. 2019. *Introduction to women's and gender studies*. New York: Oxford University Press.

Harackiewicz, Judith M., et al. 2016. Closing achievement gaps with a utility-value intervention: Disentangling race and social class. *Journal of Personality and Social Psychology* 111: 745–765. *EBSCOhost*. https://doi.org/10.1037/pspp0000075.

Hyde, Janet, et al. 2019. The future of sex and gender in psychology: Five challenges to the gender binary. *American Psychologist* 74: 171–193.

Kernahan, Cyndi. 2019. *Teaching about race and racism in the college classroom: Notes from a White Professor Morgantown*. Morgantown, WV: West Virginia University Press.

Kirk, Gwyn, and Margo Okazawa-Rey. 2019. *Gendered lives: intersectional perspectives*, 7th ed. New York: Oxford University Press.

Land, Ray, Glynis Cousin, Jan H.F. Meyer, and Peter Davies. 2005. Threshold concepts and troublesome knowledge (3): Implications for course design and evaluation. In *Improving student learning diversity and inclusivity*, ed. C. Rust, 53–64. Oxford: Centre for Staff and Learning Development.

Launius, Christie, and Holly Hassel. 2018. *Threshold concepts in women's and gender studies*. New York: Routledge.

Miller, Claire Cain. 2019. 'It doesn't have to be this way': Why some boys can keep up with girls at school. *New York Times*, January 15.

National Academies of Sciences, Engineering, and Medicine. 2018. *How people learn II: Learners, contexts, and cultures*. Washington, DC: The National Academies Press. https://doi.org/10.17226/24783.

Parker, Kim, Nikki Graf, and Ruth Igielnik. 2019. Generation Z looks a not like millennials on key social and political issues. Pew Research Center, January 17. https://www.pewsocialtrends.org/2019/01/17/generation-z-looks-a-lot-like-millennials-on-key-social-and-political-issues/.

Parkins, Ilya. 2016. Agendas, horizons, and the Canadian introductory reader: A review essay. *Atlantis* 37: 68–75.

Sapiro, Virginia. 2003. *Women in American society: An introduction to women's studies*, 5th ed. New York: McGraw-Hill.

Shaw, Susan, and Janet Lee. 2019. *Gendered voices, feminist visions: Classic and contemporary readings*, 6th ed. New York: Oxford University Press.

Taylor, Verta, Nancy Whittier, and Leila Rupp. 2019. *Feminist frontiers*. Lanham, MD: Rowman and Littlefield.

Wade, Lisa. 2013. American men's hidden crisis: They need more friends! *Salon*, December 8.

Winkler, Barbara Scott, and Carolyn DiPalma (eds.). 1999. *Teaching introduction to women's studies: Expectations and strategies*. Westport, CT: Bergin and Garvey.

4

Student Learning and Principles for Assessment

In this chapter, we delve into the questions that emerge at the assignment level, at the course level, and to a lesser extent, at the program level, regarding assessment. How do we know whether and to what extent students have achieved the learning goals and learning outcomes for the course? This chapter defines assessment at multiple levels, offers strategies for designing effective assessments, and shares some of what we have learned through our teaching and research about assessing student learning in introductory WGS courses.

This chapter will ask and offer answers to these questions: What constitutes evidence of student learning? What does student learning look like? What does student "not-learning" look like? What sorts of assignments will best help instructors assess whether and to what extent students have achieved the learning outcomes they have designed their course around? And finally, how can we use the insights we glean from analyzing our students' work to further refine and revise our course materials, our pedagogical strategies, and our means of assessing student learning? In other words, how can assessment be used in our quest to become better teachers and improve our students' learning? Our answers to these questions will come from the findings of our Scholarship of Teaching and Learning (SoTL) project, with data gathered from our respective introductory courses.

© The Author(s), under exclusive license to Springer Nature
Switzerland AG 2021
H. Hassel et al., *A Guide to Teaching Introductory Women's and Gender Studies*,
https://doi.org/10.1007/978-3-030-71785-8_4

4.1   Assessment(s) Defined

For many faculty, their first exposure to assessment might come from a "small a" level assessment that includes discussions about how they assess student learning or achievement of course goals in their individual classroom. Assessment might be conflated with grading, or it can be predetermined by a department or program-level instrument. For faculty in professional and vocational programs, assessment practices can be dictated by accrediting bodies specific to their field, as in nursing or engineering. For new instructors, assessment of student learning can be one of the most challenging parts of their classroom work, because designing authentic assessments that measure growth and proficiency rather than compliance with superficial demonstrations of academic ability require careful construction and continual revision.

In this chapter, we describe some principles that can be used to direct instructors' choices about how and what to assess, and how these decisions can and should flow from the instructor and disciplinary values. Assessments take many forms—they can be objective, like multiple choice exams or quizzes, or more subjective, like essays and open-ended responses. First, we want to borrow slightly from the assessment literature to encourage readers to think strategically about whether the assessments you design for courses are valid and reliable, while also aligned with your pedagogical goals and keyed to the course learning outcomes. Second, instructors need to think about how they're going to approach assessment in both *formative* and *summative* ways.

We don't want to rehearse the assessment or psychometrics literature here, but do think a familiarity with some of the underpinning concepts of assessment can be useful for instructors to think about:

- **Formative**: Formative assessments are those that are provided to students to use for improving their understanding or performance during the process of learning. Examples of formative assessments include low-stakes quizzes that receive corrective feedback from the instructor or auto-graded quizzes in a learning management system which are then followed by a subsequent opportunity to perform that same task or knowledge of information or skill. From the instructor's perspective, formative assessments are intended to provide a baseline and help them gauge a sense of where a learner or group of learners is at a particular point, information that can be then be used to shape subsequent instruction. If a formative assessment shows that many students are struggling to grasp a particular concept, the instructor can then provide focused instruction or activities about that particular bottleneck or roadblock before engaging in summative feedback.

- **Summative**: A summative assessment is one that concludes the period of learning and that is intended to "evaluate student learning, knowledge, proficiency, or success at the conclusion of an instructional period, like a unit, course, or program" (Yale 2021). This kind of assessment can take many forms—traditional methods like tests or exams, papers, projects, presentations, or discussions.
- **Valid Assessments are those that measure what they say they are measuring.** For example, a writing assignment might be intended to gauge students' understanding of causality, but if it is assessed on compliance with standard edited English rather than on the specified learning outcome, then that is not a valid assessment.
- **Reliable assessments measure the stated outcome consistently across populations or artifacts of student learning.** In traditional assessment literature, if, for example, the historical analysis essay is not able to be consistently assessed across artifacts or readers, then it is not reliable. As we discuss later, the issues of validity and reliability can have unique considerations within the socially-engaged classroom.

For our own project (as we annotate in Chapter 5), we focused on summative assessments, those that were used at the end of a unit of study. The first model we suggest is one that asks students to analyze an artifact (a reading, a video clip, a visual image, etc.) using course terms and frameworks as a lens. This followed, in our project, a series of classroom discussions, readings, and shorter writing assignments that are lower stakes and provide opportunities for students to "try out" new information and ideas before being asked to demonstrate their understanding by applying it to a new context. These we considered summative because they close out a unit that then becomes a foundation for the next unit of study (in the threshold concepts approach).

We also provide a number of discussion prompts in Chapter 5, which we use as formative assessments. Discussion prompts are intended to begin to surface students' understanding and provide an opportunity for peers and the instructor to "try out" new ideas, content, and application of concepts—they are also a place to identify points of misunderstanding, or probe the depth of understanding of students.

Other assessments can include formative and summative tasks that ask students to reflect on their learning and cultivate a metacognitive awareness of their learning. These types of assessments are consistent with the threshold concepts approach to teaching and more generally are a part of our desire to move away from a "coverage" model and toward structuring our courses to invite students to adopt the ways of seeing, thinking, and knowing that are valued by practitioners in the field. Quizzes are both formative and summative in that they assess students' understanding of given chapter content, but also help the instructor see what needs additional feedback and correction in the discussion (specifically in an online course) or through additional lecture or announcement material provided to students. Likewise, a unit reflection paper can provide reflective content on both the learning process (thus supporting students' *self-assessment* skills) as well as content and skill acquisition.

In the end, most of us work in a structure where teaching and learning benefits from ongoing assessment as a way to "check in" with how students are receiving and understanding material and developing new skills—but it is also the way we assign credit and grades for a course. We discuss this more at length later in the chapter, but want to note here that ensuring that the weight and proportion of *what* is being assessed is closely aligned with the outcomes for the course and program is essential, as we discussed in Chapter 2.

4.2   Reclaiming Assessment

Higher education in the United States has been increasingly marked by a culture of assessment since the 1980s. Particularly in the early years of this shift, WGS practitioners were suspicious and skeptical of assessment, often viewing it, in Caryn McTighe Musil's words, as a "judgmental tool of punishment" in which WGS programs were repeatedly called upon to justify their existence and prove their worthiness for inclusion in the curriculum (p. 4). In "Assessment and Feminist Pedagogy," Jodi Wetzel gets at what might be the heart of the matter, in providing historical context for the rise of course-level and program-level assessment in higher education. According to Wetzel, the culture of assessment in higher education can be traced back to the 1980s right-wing attacks that decried "grade inflation, dumbing down of the curriculum, and a disregard of the various traditional disciplinary canons" (1999, p. 99) and demanded various kinds of accountability measures that amounted to "intrusive external monitoring of higher education" (1999, p. 100). As both Wetzel and Musil attest, for many feminist educators, the topic of assessment is difficult to separate from the circumstances of its inception in higher education.

A different, but not unrelated kind of resistance came from those who dismissed the ability of "administratively mandated, quantitative, bureaucratically administered assessment instruments" to reveal anything meaningful about student learning in WGS courses and programs of study (Mayberry and Rose 1999, p. xi). The undergirding principles of assessment, particularly assessment that has relied on standardized ways of judgment and knowing, and purportedly quantitative or objective measurements of learning, have certainly been the site of critique and resistance by feminist instructors. This is in part because the epistemology and ethos of the feminist classroom tend to be intentionally structured in ways that may defy standardized ways of measurement, or that develop less easily assessable growth in process skills, dispositions, and habits of mind. In "Questions for a New Century: Women's Studies and Integrative Learning," Amy Levin gives voice to this concern when she recalls attending an assessment workshop at which she was instructed that "anything that could not be measured was not worth assessing" (2007, p. 29). She continues, "This dictum violated my convictions that what was most valuable about learning in Women's Studies, such as students' increased perceptions of agency and civic engagement, were difficult if not impossible to measure, particularly in the short term" (p. 29). This is to say that there is a long and valid tradition of feminist resistance to program-level assessment, and some of the learning goals for WGS courses may not be conducive to, or even be desirable to, design assessment strategies for.

These concerns persist to the present day for many; Levin's report, referenced above, was published in 2007, and she noted at that time a "continuing feminist distrust of assessment, or at least of certain models of assessment" (p. 28). The tide may be starting to turn, however; Christie organized a roundtable discussion on assessment at the 2018 NWSA Program Administrators and Directors pre-conference, and though she encountered a continuing distrust and critique of assessment, she also found an increasing number of program directors and department chairs who spoke excitedly and enthusiastically about their efforts to incorporate robust and meaningful program-level assessment practices at their respective institutions. Many of those directors and chairs spoke of a change of opinion that echoed Musil's transition from "cool wariness about assessment to warmly embracing its possibilities," (p. 4) a transition that followed on the heels of realizing that it "could indeed generate invaluable data about women's studies and student learning that would answer questions not only for skeptics but also for women's studies professors" (p. 3).

This longstanding feminist distrust of assessment has meant that though there is an amazingly rich body of scholarship on feminist pedagogy and student learning in the field of women's and gender studies, very little of that scholarship attends to the evaluation of student learning in terms of knowledge and skills, whether at the program/department level or the course level. The major exceptions in terms of large-scale program assessment and assessment of student learning are *The Courage to Question: Women's Studies and Student Learning* and *Students at the Center: Feminist Assessment,* both of which were published in 1992 and represented the tangible outcomes of a three-year research project headed by Caryn McTighe Musil, who served for six years as the executive director of the National Women's Studies Association. The research project was funded by the Department of Education's Fund for the Improvement of Postsecondary Education.[1] A slightly different vein of research during the 90s and aughts focused on gauging student growth and changes in attitudes toward the course subject matter not through an analysis of students' written work, performance on course assessments, or interviews with students, but rather through the use of survey instruments administered during the first and then again during the last week of class.[2] And finally, in the last decade, a small number of scholars in WGS have undertaken Scholarship of Teaching and Learning (SoTL) projects to study student learning, including the project that informs our understanding of student learning in this book.[3]

Our perspective is that assessment, both at the course level and the program or department level, is a key component of effective instruction. We're in agreement with the American Association of Higher Education's "Principles of Good Practice for Assessing Student Learning" that "The assessment of student learning begins with educational values. Assessment is not an end in itself but a vehicle for educational improvement. Its effective practice, then, begins with and enacts a vision of the kinds of learning we most value for students and strive to help them achieve. Educational values should drive not only what we choose to assess but also how we do so" (1992, p. 2). Throughout this book, we've emphasized some of the core values that

---

[1] See also Wetzel's "Assessment and Feminist Pedagogy" (1999), which describes assessment efforts at Metropolitan State College of Denver, and Patterson and McCulley's "An Instrument for Assessment of Women's Studies Programs," published in *Feminist Teacher* in 1997. For a more recent description of one program's efforts to implement assessment using discipline-specific learning outcomes for the purposes of improving instruction and student learning, see Van Slooten, et al., "Assessing Student Learning in Gender, Sexuality, and Women's Studies: Curricular and Faculty Development in the Two-Year College."

[2] For a review of this literature, see, for example, Macalister's "Women's Studies Classes and Their Influence on Student Development" (1999); Stake, Sevelius, and Hanly's "Student Responsiveness to Women's and Gender Studies Classes: The Importance of Student Attitudes and Classroom Relationships" (2008) both reviews the previous literature and contributes to it.

[3] See Simoes and Gray (2008), Hassel et al. (2011), and Hassel and Launius (2017).

are integral to WGS and other socially engaged fields, as well as characteristics of feminist pedagogy. Whether it's the community, empowerment, and leadership that Carolyn Shrewsbury describes in her landmark essay, "What Is Feminist Pedagogy?" (1993) or the pedagogical value of co-constructed knowledge, we believe that instructors and programs can create methods of assessment that are meaningful to students, and produce new understandings of what is happening in our classrooms so that it can be improved and shared.

4.3 Building on Pedagogy and Curriculum

The first chapters in this book invite you to build a foundational structure, one that reflects your values, the needs of the student population in the specific context in which you teach, and that uses pedagogical approaches aligned with the course learning goals and outcomes. Chapter 3, in particular, outlines some of the learning roadblocks, misconceptions, and common barriers to student understanding of the course material. As you think about how you want to assess student learning, consider the following:

- Where students start, what their prior learning experiences have been, and the specific context in which you teach and the student populations served.
- The material you have provided, ensuring that you are aligning what the explicit purpose of the material is with what is being assessed; for example, it can be easy to assign activities or material for the course with a stated goal but have an implicit assumption about what students are supposed to take away from it, perhaps a structural or abstract concept that is apparent to experts but remains challenging for those new to the field.
- Work to ensure that your assessments are aligned with the course outcome. For example, as an instructor, you might believe that participation in collaborative decision-making is important, but then not transparently factor it into group projects or discussions. In other words, if you believe something is an important skill, disposition, habit of mind, or concept, then account for it in the course evaluation system.

Table 4.1 offers some examples of alignment between types of course learning outcomes, examples of those outcomes, and some heuristic questions to ask when designing activities and assessments.

Table 4.1 Course learning outcomes, examples, and considerations for designing assessment activities

Type of course outcome	Examples	Assessment strategies and considerations
Analysis skills	using gender or other identities as a category of analysis; constructing arguments; engaging with research; interpreting sources	*Does my assessment tool ask students to define, summarize, or apply these? Multiple choice or closed-ended quiz and exam questions, for example, can lend themselves to potentially demonstrating only low levels of basic comprehension rather than more advanced thinking skills.* *What can I do to ensure that students are doing more than basic recall, or summarizing readings? If I am asking students to recall, process a new piece of evidence or artifact, and apply a theory or concept, is it manageable within the time frame I've set aside?*

Type of course outcome	Examples	Assessment strategies and considerations
Content-based learning outcomes	gendered construction of knowledge, standpoint theory, history of feminist movements	*These types of outcomes, as in many fields, can lend themselves to more objective types of assessment, including reading quizzes, short in-class writing activities, or tests that ask students to apply or understand the content, theory, or information. That being said, avoid assessments that ask for information summary without really assessing students' complete understanding of the material. For example, defining a concept will be less helpful at demonstrating students' grasp than defining and applying.*

(continued)

Table 4.1 (continued)

Type of course outcome	Examples	Assessment strategies and considerations
Dispositions/Habits of Mind	feminist curiosity; empathy	*Dispositions, such as open-mindedness, engagement, or perspective-taking, require careful consideration when designing activities or projects that will help instructors assess how effectively students are demonstrating them. Assessment prompts might, for example, ask students to consider and evaluate multiple perspectives on a given issue. A different approach would be to provide a reflective writing prompt that asks students to consider (and provide evidence for) their growth in these areas over the course of the semester).*
Ways of Knowing, Seeing, and Thinking (threshold concepts)	intersectionality, privilege and oppression, social construction of gender; praxis	*Student achievement of these typically requires in-depth assessments that involve applying a conceptual lens to a new artifact, scenario, or data set.*

Type of course outcome	Examples	Assessment strategies and considerations
Process	communicating, developing a democratic group process, cooperative learning	*These are best assessed in contexts that are active and that can be documented in some way. For example, Google docs, discussion boards in a learning management system, etc., are two ways of doing a direct assessment of the degree to which students are demonstrating these skills. Secondarily, if students are working together on a major project, having them submit a reflection or self-assessment about the group dynamic, their collaboration strategies, etc., can be another (indirect) way of assessing these skills.*
Praxis	integrative learning, applying content and process knowledge to settings outside the classroom	*Activities best suited for assessing these skills are those that ask students to take their learning "outside of the classroom walls" through action research or other project that requires them to demonstrate a complete understanding of the course material in a new context.*

4.4 Recommendations for Designing Effective Assessments

We highly recommend trying to gauge students' starting points at the beginning of the semester; doing so can be a rich source of information, and can provide the instructor with a picture of whether, where, and at what depth students have previously encountered course concepts and frameworks. You might also be able to get a sense of how the personal is political for the students and the kind of emotional terrain that they bring with them to the classroom. Use that information, be guided by that information, and yet stay open to the possibilities of student growth and transformation, i.e., don't forget your pedagogy of invitation. As we have discussed throughout the book, recognizing and working with students' divergent entry points can be a powerful aid in designing and teaching a successful intro-level course. Whenever possible, design assessments that take this wide variation into account. This doesn't mean necessarily grading in a comparative versus absolute way but rather working to account for the perspectives and backgrounds that students bring to the classroom.

When designing formative assessments in particular, we recommend aiming to design assignments that will allow students to both demonstrate what they've learned AND simultaneously build on that learning (for example, reflective journals, discussions, and essays). We also recommend being transparent with students that you're asking them to link and make connections between their personal experiences and larger structural systems, by locating themselves within those larger structures. When possible, model what that might look like. Affective or dispositional growth comes from the exercise of reframing a past experience through the conceptual framework of the course. The hope is that students then form a richer understanding of themselves, which provides an effective foundation upon which to build for the rest of the course and beyond.

As we have discussed throughout the book, adopting and employing a macro-level perspective is a heavy lift for many students in the course, and keeping that in mind when designing assessments can be helpful. When discussing assignments in class and when creating assignment sheets, it is probably wise to remind students about the distinction between response to and analysis of texts, images, films, etc., and to be clear about whether you're asking students to provide both, and in what proportion. Relatedly, because some students perceive that WGS instructors assign grades on the basis of a student's political position, instructors may want to design assessments that foreground having students demonstrate their understanding of key concepts, as opposed to their response to or position on various issues. As with so many of the aspects of the introductory course that we have discussed, there is no one right way to do this; instead, our point here is to advocate for being deliberate and intentional with your choices.

When designing both formative and summative assessments, we believe transparency is of utmost importance. Whenever possible, make your assessment criteria visible (and then, of course, adhere to those criteria when assessing students' work). For example, use rubrics that spell out what *different levels of performance look like* (see Chapter 5 for examples), provide guidelines that spell out what excellent performance looks like, or give students models, as well as opportunities to talk through the qualities of the models. This is not to say that this is an easy task; it can be difficult, even for seasoned instructors, to surface and explicitly articulate what it is we are looking for in students' work, and to put into words what the expectations or benchmarks are for average, above average, and excellent demonstration of the assessment's learning outcomes. In our experience, this work has been made easier by engaging in periodic norming sessions with colleagues. In these types of sessions, we read and assess sample student work using a rubric, and then discuss why we assessed it the way we did.

In Chapter 2, we discussed the importance of attaching value (in terms of the relative weight given different assessments) in ways that are aligned with the stated course learning goals and outcomes. We return to that issue here as a reminder to keep it in mind as you are designing your overall course assessment structure. For example, if you value process skills and students' ability to grapple with complex ideas and different people, then the weight that is attached to class discussion (online or f2f), collaborative projects, and informal writing should be significant, (perhaps 25–30%) with accompanying levels of specificity about what strong learning looks like in this area. Students make rational and materially-grounded choices about what they put their time and energy into, because both are limited resources. If an instructor says they value having students grapple with complex ideas and that they want students to learn to collaborate with others, but 90% of the grade is on timed exams, then students will make choices about where to spend the most time accordingly.

4.5   Evaluating Student Work

First, a word about grades in relation to this discussion of assessment of student learning. In the best of all possible worlds, a students' grade in a course is a reflection of their learning vis-à-vis the stated course goals and expectations. There are many instances when this is not the case, however; perhaps a student didn't turn in all the assignments, and a zero on one or more assignments resulted in an overall lower grade, even though the work they turned in was strong and the student in other ways demonstrated that they learned a lot in the course. Or perhaps the student's grade was negatively impacted by their poor attendance, in that their frequent absences made it more difficult to acquire the content knowledge and skills that were the focus of the course, and this was reflected in their work. In general, we believe that assessment models that assign grades, for example, primarily on the basis of attendance (as distinct from the scenario described above), or on standard written English, miss important opportunities to anchor evaluation practices squarely in learning and proficiency rather than on behavioral characteristics that can disproportionately impact minoritized and vulnerable students, and those with significant material barriers to college access.

On a related note, one of the frustrations we have experienced as instructors over the years is in regards to students whose learning seems to plateau. Put differently, we have noted that some students come into the class with a solid baseline of knowledge and skills, but seem to "coast" rather than engaging deeply with the course material and pushing their knowledge and skills to a new level. We were reminded of this phenomenon in the context of analyzing our SoTL data, which entailed reading all the work produced over the course of the semester by an individual student in one sitting. There was, of course, quite a bit of variation among the students in terms of their progress or gains, but there were a number of students who started the semester strong, but then seemed to stall and stay in stasis throughout the remainder of the course. In the end, we can only speculate on why this is so. We believe that many of the students we would place in this category are making rational choices based on time management and where their limited energy and resources need to be directed. As instructors, we may be irritated to see them not really push themselves, but on the other hand, perhaps we need to respect that this is an imminently reasonable choice, a means to an end, etc.[4]

---

[4]Recent emerging assessment trends like contract grading, labor-based contract grading, and "ungrading" are efforts on the part of faculty across disciplines to more accurately account for and encourage student learning and growth (see Melzer et al.; Inoue 2019; Stommel 2018).

In contrast to the students who "coast," for whatever reason, are the students who make significant learning gains over the course of the semester but whose written work is rather unpolished, not in spite of, but *because* of these gains. This insight also emerged in re-reading student work in the context of our SoTL project, months removed from the time-bound pressures of assigning course grades. We were struck by how what we came to call "raggedy" writing frequently shows strong evidence of student learning. A frequent assumption is that student writing that is a "mess," i.e., unclearly written, poorly organized, containing logical inconsistencies, and/or not as tightly focused as we would like, is evidence that a student hasn't learned. However, we would like to suggest that in this student writing, there is often simultaneously strong evidence of active, sustained engagement and grappling with the course material. More specifically, sometimes students' writing is "raggedy" precisely *because* they are actively grappling with new and unfamiliar concepts and frameworks and are in a liminal learning space. One way to acknowledge this aspect of student learning is to build on assessment criteria that value evidence of active engagement with the course concepts. In addition, instructors might choose to de-emphasize, or selectively emphasize, the importance of polished prose in their assessment criteria. We advocate developing your skill at "reading" student work, and being able to make student learning (or the lack thereof) visible to you.

4.6 Making Student Learning Visible: Charting Growth in Learning Domains

In this section, we offer examples from our research into student achievement of the threshold concepts, linking the learning roadblocks identified in Chapter 3 with examples from our students' work in order to show what student learning (and students' struggles to learn) might look like as you assess your own students' work. We will focus on how some of the common learning roadblocks might show up (or might be overcome) in a writing assignment or exam. More broadly, we return to the common learning roadblocks we identified in the previous chapter in order to suggest that instructors keep them in mind when designing assessments and then subsequently evaluating them, as summative assessments can be a place to gauge whether or to what extent students have navigated through them.

Misconceptions about the Field and Liminality: Though some textbooks for introductory courses will directly address misconceptions about the field, it can be a semester-long process for some students to confront or disabuse themselves of these misconceptions. Miley, for example, wrote in her reflective essay that "Before the class started I was skeptical on how I was going to like the class and what it was really about," but goes on to say that "When the class started I was very surprised, in a good way." As a working-class white woman, Miley found much in the course material that resonated with her experience, and her level of engagement with the course material was highest when engaging with issues that directly related to her personal experience, as indicated when she wrote "Yeah this section [on privilege and oppression] hit on a really personal level, but I love it because I was able to understand it that much better then." At the same time, she also brought with her into the class a strong attachment to "bootstraps" and meritocratic ideology, in ways that made it more difficult for her to cross the threshold of understanding with regard to economic inequality. We point again to Miley's example to draw attention to the ways that students' movement through (in our course structure) threshold concepts like privilege and oppression, intersectionality, and the social construction of gender can be uneven. Looking at the work she produced over the course of the semester, we found significant evidence of learning and growth, even as her understanding of several key course concepts was still at a developmental level. As instructors, it can be useful to think about both uneven movement and levels of growth or movement that are significant for that student but that may still fall short of the mark that we would ideally like to see, and how to take these into account when assessing student learning.

Essentialism: As we noted in Chapter 3, some students struggle as they move toward a social constructionist understanding of gender and away from essentialist understandings of sex and gender. Student examples from Skills Assessment 1 in our research project help illustrate this. One student, Krystal, wrote this analysis of the first prompt on the phenomenon of gender-reveal parties: "Gender Reveal parties are stating that gender is static and unchanging, that there is nothing more than a boy and a girl. They are reinforcing the idea of gender essentialism which says that boys and girls are opposite and promotes a fixed notion of gender." Krystal's analysis is suggestive of a critical understanding of the gender binary. By contrast, we have also seen students who demonstrate understanding that gender is constructed as a binary and readily grant that there are more than two genders, only to write with conviction that there really *are* only two sexes. A different kind of example comes from Sierra, who, when responding to the prompt about gender-reveal parties, used one paragraph to describe what they are and the other paragraph to offer ahistorical assertions about them that reveal a conflation between sex and gender: "Since before I was born, it has always been you usually determine the sex of the baby by girls being pink and boys being the color blue. Society has always been this way and I think as we keep getting older and society is changing we will soon see that Gender reveal parties will turn into Sex reveal parties." Sierra's final sentence suggests that calling these parties "gender reveal" is a misnomer, though this is not explicitly stated, much less explored.

Another consideration in accounting for essentialism is a tendency toward generalization that some students may demonstrate. For example, one student, Ursula, early in her writing made claims like "Our culture is one big binary" and "All in all this commercial is stupid." In the same assessment, she unpacked the bathroom image as follows:

> When I look at this I see what looks to be a boy that is confused about their gender identity and they are looking at either dressing how they feel and getting yelled at or acting as their projected gender and getting beat up for not acting like a boy. Or you could look at this as a girl with short hair that is also confused and is either looking at dressing as what they want to be and getting beat up for not being a boy or dressing as their projected gender and getting yelled at for not acting like a girl. Either way there is conflict because of the binaries.

We see Ursula making some important progress in the complexity of her language and thinking, but also note that she may not be at the level of sophistication, at the start, that some other students with greater levels of college-level and rhetorical literacies might be. More specifically, in analyzing the image, Ursula grasps that the person pictured is presented with binary options with regard to gender, but she does not take the further step to assert that sex and gender are not, in fact, binaries. As you design assessments, we recommend thinking about what degree, level, and kinds of progress signal benchmark levels of achievement and how to account for those messy learning processes that can happen over time.

Three interconnected learning roadblocks that we introduced in Chapter 3 are what we call **"Response v. analysis," "Struggles with New Language,"** and **"Attachment to the Known."** We treat them here together because they can manifest in similar ways. One of the teaching and learning goals for each of these three areas is to encourage students to develop critical literacy and move past clichés or editorial commentary into analysis. Any kind of assessment task that asks students to analyze is likely to elicit some typical responses. For example, students may feel the need to offer an emotional response to or pass judgment on issues like racism or sexism, as Sandra does, noting: "Sadly, this is America." Students may also use language that is hyperbolic or that passes judgment rather than being analytical, as in this example from Gwen, who uses the charged verb "glorifies" in her discussion: "The elements of privilege and oppression that are being discussed in 'Poor Kids Who do Everything Right Don't Do Better Than Rich Kids Who Do Everything Wrong' is glorified toward one side. The one side being rich kids who have everything handed to them. The article glorifies rich kids as legacies." This quote from Gwen also seems to indicate a misreading, in that she appears not to understand that the article is revealing meritocracy to be a myth rather than glorifying the status quo.

Students like Julius and Colleen show examples of the oft-used and loaded word "degrading," used frequently by students in lieu of analytical terms: "Whether the intent of the advertisement was to degrade women seems very debatable," writes Julius, while Colleen observes "not only why this video degrades women to nothing more than beautiful, empty shells, but why is there an image of a man throwing things and destroying porcelain male figurines." We have noted a pattern of students using this particular term, and we agreed that it stands out to us because it is not a term that we ourselves use, nor do the course readings. As an instructor then, it is important to *expect* imprecision in analytical language from students who are new to the discipline, and often to the intellectual task of analysis. Direct instruction and modeling of analytical language can be helpful, and feedback on formative assessments about how language reflects rhetorical function can be steps toward helping students deepen their analysis skills.

It's also important to account for the ways that learning is reflected in both new language and in the ways that students may grapple with particular ideological attachments that the course content can challenge. For example, one of our participating students, Tracy, produced skills assessments showing this intellectual work. In their analysis of trans identity, Tracy refers to a "woman who identifies as a man" and uses feminine pronouns rather than using the terminology of "trans man" and masculine pronouns. It is important to recognize that language relating to trans identity is very new for many students and keep this in mind when evaluating students' work. Later, Tracy relies heavily on their understanding of police as protectors and servants, concluding in Skills Assessment 2 that "Thankfully in this scenario, the patrol car officer saw that this was injustice and respectively allowed the man to leave freely. This officer apologized for the inconvenience and gave contact information. This shows not everyone abuses privilege and with the right individuals, it can turn to good results." This is less analysis than overreach into gratitude and an emotional attachment to an image of law enforcement and justice that isn't necessarily shown in the video clip the student watched. Instructors can both acknowledge students' attachments to familiar ideologies and language and simultaneously press them for more complex considerations of course material.

A final note about students' struggles with new language in relation to assessment focuses on the logistical incorporation of course terms and frameworks into their writing. For example, students' struggles to understand intersectionality frequently manifest in their writing as awkward and/or imprecise usages of the term. In her analysis of maternal mortality through an intersectional lens in Skills Assessment 3, Tanya demonstrates her accurate understanding of how race and class affect women's likelihood of dying during childbirth, even as she struggles to incorporate the terminology into her own words, writing of "many mothers of all intersections" and "one of the intersections Black mothers face." In her reflective essay, she writes of "how to look beyond gender and see someone's intersectionality." In assessing work like this, we try to affirm the student's progress even as we offer encouragement to continue working on how to deepen their understanding in ways that will eventually manifest in smoothed-out language. For some students, these awkward or imprecise usages of course concepts are accompanied by an over-reliance on quotes from course material. While we explicitly ask students to provide evidence from the course material in the form of paraphrase and/or direct quotes in support of their analysis, we mostly see students rely too heavily on direct quotes when they are unable to demonstrate understanding of course concepts and frameworks in their own words.

In addition to identifying some of the common ways that students get "stuck" and encounter barriers to their understanding, we have also taken note of some strategies that seem to facilitate a greater and deeper understanding of the course material. In Chapter 3, we discussed these issues under the heading of **"Supporting Transfer" and "Cultivating Metacognition,"** and bring them up here because they both also have implications for assessment. Both of these areas have been of significant interest to scholars of assessment generally and writing assessment particularly in the last decade. What we want to draw attention to here are the kinds of assessment opportunities that can be most helpful to encourage students to do "near" and "far" transfer (between closely related contexts and less-closely related contexts). For example, we observed throughout our project how effectively students were able to integrate new understandings of the threshold concepts when they made connections to their *future occupational and professional aspirations.* We saw this repeatedly, an example of which is found in Josefina's reflective essay: "The skills I acquired in this course this semester will greatly help me with my career as a social worker. I acquired the skill of being a better advocate. This is because of all the material I learned about a variety of populations. The information will help me understand the oppression going on in people's lives. The terms and concepts we learned will also help me when interacting with clients." Zuzu, as well, made connections to her future work as a nurse, writing: "I want to be the kind of nurse that always advocates for her patients and listens to them thoroughly, this class has taught me how to better understand my future patients' struggles. I want to be the understanding and caring nurse that can make one area in my patient's life just a little less hard with making sure their problems are my main priority." Another student, Kevin, reflected in his final essay that

> This class has offered a lot to me that I can apply to my future career in law enforcement. It has reinforced a lot of the things I already knew and shown me new things that I had never considered before. The goal of law enforcement is to serve and protect the people. In many cases, the police have shown that they are failing to do that. Discriminating against the oppressed populations. This class has given me the background information to change the norm and treat all people equally.

Assessments, then, that invite these kinds of connections can be an especially useful tool in ensuring that students' learning is deep and long-lasting rather than short-term.

Metacognition, as well, or students' awareness of their own learning and how they are understanding or not understanding new concepts, should be encouraged as part of any instructor's assessment strategies. We want to emphasize that this can be *both* students identifying the extent to which they have grasped a new idea *and* how or when they have not. This kind of meta-awareness is critical to new learning and growth. For example, Lotte writes in her Skills Assessment 3 response:

> I feel like Jimmy Kimmel was making fun of Lil Wayne and he was kind of rude to him, but I thought that's how his show is, and that's how he always does it. Honestly, I am not sure what I should have seen in the interview. It felt like Lil Wayne was being attacked/targeted and it was not comfortable to watch, not at all, and he is a wildly successful man. When they talked about him losing his virginity I was most uncomfortable, he was only 11 and a 14 year old girl basically forced herself on him and he said it kind of messed him up but it was still a joke to everyone. I know, this is not a very high quality answer, but I really do not understand what I was supposed to be seeing and understanding from that clip.

This student struggled to understand racialized masculinity and even though she was not able to make this leap, she also has an important tool that can be critical to an instructor's intervention, in that she recognizes something is missing from her analysis. More specifically, in her narration of her affective response to watching the clip, she provides valuable information to the instructor about where she is at in her learning. In fact, the student hones in on what we agree is one of the key moments in the interview vis-à-vis course concepts and makes clear through her description of her discomfort that she recognizes that this is the heart of the matter. While she falls short of being able to offer polished (or even ragged) analysis, she clearly demonstrates that she is engaged with the material and is on the cusp of getting there.

Gloria, too, demonstrates developing skills of metacognition: "Intersectionality was probably the hardest threshold concept for me to wrap my head around. It takes all of the previous things we learned and rolls it all up into one." We point here to Gloria's recognition that "I know there are things I don't know here" which shows a kind of awareness as she processes her course learning in her reflective essay. This, we think, speaks to the value of working to create an assessment space that *values learning and growth as much as understanding*. We encourage instructors to be aware of the ways that they are creating a learning environment where students are able to document how their learning has been facilitated or stalled, and what barriers they themselves see in their ability to work through the course concepts and material.

Last, we draw attention to two specific kinds of thinking and learning that can be the most challenging to account for in assessment, **macro-level thinking and affective dimensions of learning**. As we have discussed throughout the book, one of the primary goals—in our judgment—in the women's and gender studies classroom (or other socially engaged fields) is helping students move from micro- to macro-levels of thinking. In part this can be both the language of macro-understandings of institutions and systems, and specific demonstration of examples that show these. For example, Krystal writes in her third skills assessment that "These [sexism and male privilege] occur because of the ideology that women are sluts or whores if they engage in sexual activities and men are praised for doing the same. This ideology is systematically embedded in society and is continuously reinforced and held by institutions and images that demonstrate male privilege." She later develops this analysis more fully, but the point we make here is that instructors who want students to show evidence of macro-level thinking can cue them with specific vocabulary as well as model how they can illustrate that understanding in their assessments. Another student, Mizumi, also demonstrated an understanding of the systemic dimensions of oppression in her second skills assessment, though the language she uses suggests that this type of understanding and analysis is new to her: "In this situation, racism and colorism are the oppression, and social institution is a police officer. However, police officers were black, so it is possible to assume that the oppression was not done by the officers but the institution." Again, though her wording is a bit awkward, she appears to be working toward an understanding of individuals in relation to social institutions, and how oppression operates through institutions and not just or only through individual actions.

Women's and gender studies courses are likely to invite students to engage in and work through affective dimensions of their learning. As we describe throughout the book, this goes well beyond questions of trigger warnings and safe spaces and into the development of particular kinds of dispositions like empathy, as well as the emotions that emerge as students learn about and work through content that may be challenging. Assessments that account for this part of the learning process may not specifically invite students to share it with the instructor but can create a space (whether through a journal, a f2f or online small group discussion, or some other venue) for students to recognize that the topics in WGS courses can tap into this. Amy, for example, spoke to this in Skills Assessment 2: "As a girls point of view, it makes me very upset that the young girl speaking even had to question reporting the post. It also disappoints me that Facebook did not take the picture off," while Jessie speaks to the gender wage gap, and identifies how the content triggered an emotional experience: "Another day that stood out to me was the day of the reading 'Motherhood Penalty Vs. Fatherhood Penalty.' I knew that men got paid more than women, but I never realized the amount of privilege that men have over women. They are not only paid more but are in general viewed as much greater than women and this is something that stood out to me due to the way it made me feel." We point to these examples in order to note, for instructors, that these are regular parts of the teaching and learning process in the WGS classroom, and that it can be, for some instructors, an uncomfortable component of their assessment practices. Certainly, beyond the examples we provide here from our research study, the three co-authors have managed a range of other affective dimensions that emerge in the learning process—including resistance, hostility, and from some students—anger. We've found that it is productive to view this complete range of emotions that instructors might encounter in the ongoing assessment process as normal and in fact potentially valuable indicators of student engagement and learning.

We'd like to close here by advocating for what in the assessment literature is called "closing the loop," which is to say, taking the insights gleaned from the assessment process and using them to revisit and revise any and all relevant aspects of your course. Most commonly, an instructor might take note of areas where a significant number of students fall short of achieving a particular learning outcome, and think about what sorts of changes in their pedagogical practice might support student learning in those areas. Conversely, an instructor might come away from the assessment process realizing that student learning is happening in an area that is not fully or explicitly accounted for in the course learning outcomes; in this instance, an instructor could revise their learning outcomes to capture that desired knowledge or skill, and also think about what sorts of course materials and/or pedagogical activities would further support learning in that area.

Overall, it is our hope that we have made a compelling case for how and why the process of assessment can provide valuable insights into student learning. It is perhaps *least* interesting to us as the process whereby we assign course grades. And of course, in the context of our work as instructors, we frequently view grading as an onerous, time-consuming chore, done under time pressure and often after a period of procrastination. We are here trying to build a bandwagon for returning to the assessments we use in our courses with a more reflective, contemplative eye, one that is an extension of our pedagogies of invitation, in that it remains open to seeing evidence of learning and growth even amidst unpolished prose and uneven and sometimes contradictory claims and arguments.

Works Cited

American Association of Higher Education. 1992. Principles of good practice for assessing student learning. https://www.learningoutcomesassessment.org/wp-content/uploads/2019/08/AAHE-Principles.pd. Accessed 18 January 2021.

Hassel, Holly, Christie Launius. 2017. Crossing the threshold in introductory women's and gender studies courses: An assessment of student learning. *Teaching & Learning Inquiry* 5 (2): 30.

Hassel, Holly, Amy Reddinger, and Jessica van Slooten. 2011. Surfacing the structures of patriarchy: Teaching and learning threshold concepts in women's studies. *International Journal for the Scholarship of Teaching and Learning* 5. Available at: https://doi.org/10.20429/ijsotl.2011.050218.

Inoue, Asao. 2019. *Labor-based grading contracts: Building equity and inclusion in the compassionate writing classroom*. WAC Clearinghouse.

Levin, Amy. 2007. Questions for a new century: Women's studies and integrative learning. Report to the National Women's Studies Association.

Mayberry, Maralee, and Ellen Cronan Rose (eds.). 1999. *Meeting the challenge: Innovative feminist pedagogies in action*. New York: Routledge.

Melzer, Daniel, et al. N.D. So your instructor is using contract grading…Writing Commons. https://writingcommons.org/article/so-your-instructor-is-using-contract-grading/. Accessed 18 January 2021.

Musil, Caryn McTighe (ed.). 1992. *Students at the center: Feminist assessment.* Association of American Colleges.

———, et al. 1992. *The courage to question: Women's studies and student learning.*

Patterson, Patricia M., and Lucretia McCulley. 1997. An instrument for feminist assessment of women's studies programs. *Feminist Teacher* 11: 39–54.

Shrewsbury, Carol. 1993. What is feminist pedagogy? *Women's Studies Quarterly* 15: 9–16.

Simoes, Solange and Suzanne Gray. 2008. Combining academic service-learning and information literacy: A new framework for an introductory Women's Studies Course. *The Scholarship of Teaching and Learning at Eastern Michigan University* 2. https://commons.emich.edu/sotl/vol2/iss1/8/.

Stommel, Jesse. 2018. How to ungrade. https://www.jessestommel.com/how-to-ungrade/. Accessed 18 January 2021.

Slooten, Van, Amy Reddinger Jessica, Holly Hassel, and Ann Mattis. 2019. Assessing student learning in gender, sexuality, and women's studies: Curricular and faculty development in the two-year college. In *Theory and praxis: Women's and gender studies at community colleges*, ed. Genevieve Carminati and Heather Relihan. Arlington, VA: Gival P.

Wetzel, Jodi. 1999. Assessment and feminist pedagogy. In *Meeting the challenge: Innovative feminist pedagogies in action*, ed. Maralee Mayberry and Ellen Cronan Rose. New York: Routledge.

Yale Poorvu Center for Teaching and Learning. 2021. Formative and summative assessments. https://poorvucenter.yale.edu/Formative-Summative-Assessments. Accessed 18 January 2021.

5

Annotated Examples of Assessments and Rubrics

As we've emphasized throughout this book, instructors have many decisions to make and contextual factors to consider when they design their courses, from the textbook to the materials to the pedagogical approach to assessment. In this chapter, we provide the assessments we used for our SoTL research project, as well as additional writing assignments, quizzes, rubrics, and discussion prompts. These have been used across our various teaching contexts, including two research-intensive universities with modestly selective admissions, regional comprehensives, and open-admissions two-year colleges.

We use a type of assignment we call "skills assessments" at regular intervals throughout the Intro course to gauge students' understanding of the threshold concepts that the course is structured around. These skills assessments ask students to use course concepts as a lens through which to analyze a variety of images, videos, and texts. We are looking not only for evidence that the students can explain these concepts in their own words, as well as through paraphrase and quotation of course materials, but also for what they can DO with those concepts, in terms of applying them analytically.

As the semester progresses, we also look for evidence that the students' understanding of the threshold concepts is deepening, and that they see the connections among them.

Assessments used during the semester (spring 2018) we collected data for our SoTL project

© The Author(s), under exclusive license to Springer Nature
Switzerland AG 2021
H. Hassel et al., *A Guide to Teaching Introductory Women's and Gender Studies*,
https://doi.org/10.1007/978-3-030-71785-8_5

Throughout the book, we have incorporated quotes from student assessments to illustrate our points about student learning in introductory WGS courses. These are the prompts the students were responding to.

5.1 Skills Assessment 1: Social Construction of Gender

Question 1: Gender reveal parties are becoming more popular in the United States. Please read the description of a typical gender-reveal party below:

> The house was filled with balloons and confetti, and the guests were decked out in team colors, ready to cheer. Minutes before the party kicked off, they eagerly cast votes on the outcome. But this festive gathering was not a Super Bowl celebration. The decorations were all in pinks and powder blues, and the sides involved were "Team Boy" and "Team Girl." This was a gender-reveal party, during which expectant parents share the moment they discover their baby's sex, unveiling results of the ultrasound test among loved ones.

Write a 2–4 paragraph analysis of the Gender-Reveal party as a cultural phenomenon. Using course concepts, how can you complicate our understanding of these parties and what they signify about our culture?[1]

Question 2: Watch the following commercial, entitled "Pretty" for Droid phones:

> http://www.youtube.com/watch?v=w83UQkiuNZQ.

Here is the text of the voiceover in the commercial:

> "Droid. Should a phone be pretty? Should it be a tiara-wearing digitally clueless beauty pageant queen? Or should it be fast? Racehorse duct-taped to a Scud missile fast. We say the latter. So we built the phone that does. Does rip through the Web like a circular saw through a ripe banana. Is it a precious porcelain figurine of a phone? In truth? No. It's not a princess. It's a robot. A phone that trades hair-do for can-do."

---

[1]This question was our first real attempt to ask skills assessment-type questions, not just exam questions. It was useful in the sense that gender-reveal parties were familiar to most students and so were a rich topic to analyze and demonstrate new language and concepts. However, the prevalence of pop feminist critiques of gender reveal parties in several online publications quickly made this question too prone to plagiarizing others' insights.

How does this ad illustrate several key concepts that we have learned about in class? Drawing from our readings and class discussions, analyze the cultural messages that this commercial reinforces. Your answer should be approximately 3–5 paragraphs in length and contain specific insights, examples, and connections.[2]

Question 3: What's going on in this image,[3] and what is the dilemma represented in it? How does this image connect to several of the key concepts that you've learned about in this unit? Your answer should be 3–5 paragraphs in length and make specific references to course material.

5.2 Skills Assessment 2: Privilege and Oppression

For this skills assessment, answer the following questions in a Word document. When you are finished, upload your document to the D2L Dropbox folder labeled "Skills 2."

Grading criteria for skills assessments:

- Do you demonstrate an accurate understanding of course concepts related to **privilege and oppression** (and the social construction of gender)?
- Do you use those course concepts to frame your analysis?
- Do you provide adequate evidence from the course material to back up your assertions and observations?
- Do you organize your thoughts into coherent, relatively error-free paragraphs?

Question 1: Watch this video clip: http://www.washingtonpost.com/posttv/local/dc-police-investigating-burglary-stop-man/2014/10/07/f3704e36-4e4c-11e4-877c-335b53ffe736_video.html.

Using course concepts, carefully analyze what is happening in this video. Your answer should be between 2 and 4 paragraphs.

Question 2: Read the article, "Poor Kids Who Do Everything Right Don't Do Better Than Rich Kids Who Do Everything Wrong" (Washington Post), and then write a response that does the following:

---

[2]This question was effective at seeing students' emerging analytical skills. Could a student analyze the voiceover and imagery of the commercial, or merely describe it? This question also was a good litmus test of students' integration of new language. Most students readily grasp that the concept of "gender ranking" would be important to discuss in their answer, while other students would rely mostly on language that they had coming into the course, i.e., that the commercial was "degrading."

[3]https://criticalmediaproject.org/transgender-bathroom-meme/.

1. Clearly identifies what elements of privilege and oppression are being discussed
2. Analyzes the article in terms of the threshold concept of privilege and oppression
3. Explicitly refers to related concepts from the chapter.

Question 3: In 2012, radio station WNYC featured a story in their Radio Rookies series about sexual cyberbullying. You can find the story here:

http://www.wnyc.org/story/259398-sexual-cyberbullying-modern-day-let ter/.

Listen carefully to the eight-minute clip and then write a 3–5 paragraph analysis of the story through the lens of the threshold concepts of privilege and oppression. You may also refer back to the social construction of gender, but the more recent material should be your main focus. In your response, be sure to explicitly refer to relevant course terms and concepts that help explain the phenomenon of sexual cyberbullying.[4]

5.3   Skills Assessment 3: Intersectionality

For this skills assessment, answer the following two questions in a Word document. Each answer should be a minimum of 500 words long, for a total of at least 1,000 words.

Grading criteria for skills assessments:

1. Do you demonstrate an accurate understanding of course concepts related to intersectionality, privilege and oppression and the social construction of gender?
2. Do you use those course concepts to frame your analysis?
3. Do you provide adequate evidence from the course material to back up your assertions and observations?
4. Do you organize your thoughts into coherent, relatively error-free paragraphs?

---

[4]This assessment question was very effective at illustrating which students were acquiring (or already had) macro-level thinking and analysis skills. Many students would only discuss the individual-level harms depicted in the story, and those same students tended to respond to the prompt by personalizing it (describing how they would feel or describing how something similar had happened to them). Students who exhibited macro-level thinking and analysis would be able to name the ideologies and institutions that contributed to what the story calls "sexual cyberbullying."

Question 1: As quoted at the beginning of Chapter 4, Estelle Freedman encourages feminists to always ask two questions: "We must always ask not only, 'What about women?' (what difference does gender make?) but also 'Which women?' (what difference do race, class, or nationality make?)." Over the last three weeks, we have read about and discussed numerous issues that emphasize the importance of asking both of these questions. Choose one of these issues and write an essay that explains what you can see and understand when you go beyond thinking about the topic solely in terms of gender, and instead employ an intersectional lens. In your response, be sure to explicitly refer to specific readings.[5]

Question 2: In 2009, Lil Wayne appeared on the Jimmy Kimmel show; news anchor Charlie Gibson is also on stage during the interview, as he was Kimmel's previous guest. Watch the clip carefully (it is on D2L) and then analyze it using an intersectional lens. You may refer back to the threshold concepts of the social construction of gender and privilege and oppression, but the more recent material should be your main focus. In your response, be sure to explicitly refer to relevant course terms and concepts that help explain what's going on in the conversation.[6]

5.4   Skills Assessment 4: Reflective Essay on Feminist Praxis

Write a 4–5 page, double-spaced essay in response to the following prompt. In writing your essay, be as specific and thorough as possible, providing quotes and paraphrase from the course material to support and explain your points. Please include a separate introduction and conclusion in your essay.

Prompt

Reflecting on your learning over the course of the semester,

---

[5]This is an example of an assessment question that honestly wasn't that effective. It was structured as a fairly typical short essay-style format and tended to elicit student responses that were rather descriptive and summaries of course readings. We discontinued this question for those reasons, because it didn't align with the student learning outcomes that we were striving for.

[6]We loved this question and were sad to retire it due to Lil Wayne's decreasing cultural relevance. This short video clip (with captions) was a fantastic test of students' intersectional analysis skills and really highlighted their development over the semester. Students frequently referred back to their "aha" insights in answering this question in their reflective essays as well. Finding a clip or image or reading that works so well is enormously difficult for lots of reasons (e.g., finding something that can't easily be googled to find a feminist critique), but it really pays off in terms of measuring student learning.

1. Describe what you have learned about each of the four threshold concepts, including the relationship between them, and
2. Describe how you might use that knowledge to engage in your communities to advocate for social justice and create a more equitable world, in ways both big and small.

I will base my assessment of your essay on the following:

- application of learning to your own life and the world around you
- critical reflection that demonstrates synthesis of ideas
- specificity of examples used to demonstrate knowledge gained and potential for future engagement
- knowledge of key terms, concepts, and readings from the course
- clearly written prose with a minimum of sentence-level errors.

5.5   Additional Skills Assessment Questions

5.5.1   Questions Focusing on the Social Construction of Gender

1. Before answering this question, please read the short first-person story by Jen Mecum, "I'm Butch and Five Months Pregnant and Yes, I'll take your subway seat" (published on NewNowNext in October 2019).

   Utilizing course concepts, how would you explain and analyze some of the struggles and insights that Mecum describes in this essay? What connections can you draw between our course readings and some of the experiences that she discusses in this essay? Your answer should be 4–6 paragraphs in length and make specific references to course material and specific course concepts.

2. A couple of years ago, a team of scientists measured the testosterone levels of 27 couples (all men partnered with women) over the course of the women's pregnancies. The picture on the left is a graph of what they found. The picture on the right is a stock image of what you might find when searching for "pregnant woman" online. **Utilizing course concepts, how can you explain what is going on in the graph and the picture? Also using course concepts, analyze how these two images are at odds with one another.** (Figs. 5.1 and 5.2)

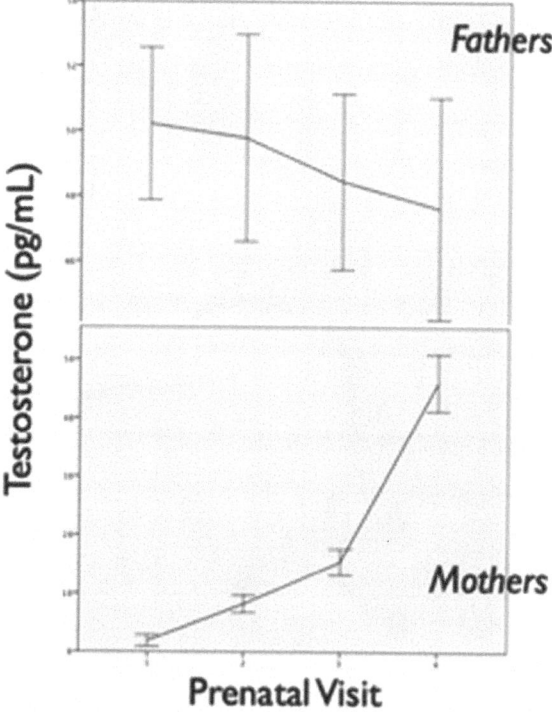

Fig. 5.1 Testosterone levels of couples over the course of women's pregnancies (*Source* "Fathers' decline in testosterone and synchrony with partner testosterone during pregnancy predicts greater postpartum relationship investment," Darby E. Saxbe, et al., *Hormones and Behavior* 90 [2017]: 42)

5.5.2 Questions Focusing on the Threshold Concepts of Privilege and Oppression

1. Watch the following short clip with actress Chloe Bennet discussing her difficulty finding acting jobs when she first came to Hollywood: https://people.com/movies/chloe-bennet-was-once-told-she-wasnt-white-enough-and-wasnt-asian-enough-for-hollywood/

   For more context about why she is speaking out about this issue lately, read this short article in Teen Vogue: https://www.teenvogue.com/story/chloe-bennet-changing-last-name

   Utilizing what you have learned in this course, write a 2–3 paragraph analysis of this story through the lens of the threshold concept of privilege and oppression.

2. The following image is a recent picture of a student who uses a wheelchair attending a lecture at their university: [image of a large lecture hall that is

Fig. 5.2 Pregnant woman (*Source* Photo by Kate Hliznitsova, Unsplash)

inaccessible with a student in a wheelchair sitting in the aisle at the back corner of the lecture hall]

Utilizing course concepts, write a 2–3 paragraph analysis of this image through the lens of privilege and oppression.

3. Imagine you are having a conversation with a friend and the Gender Wage Gap comes up. Your friend says, "The gender wage gap is just a myth. Women just need to make different career choices that pay better. As long as they get good grades, negotiate aggressively, and don't slack off when they become mothers, they'll be treated equally."

Utilizing what you have learned in this unit, write a 5–7 paragraph response. What claims might you agree or disagree with? What counterclaims would you make? What course concepts could you use to analyze this issue? How could you add nuance or complexity to this discussion?

5.6   Wildcat Voices Assignment[7]

As we've been discussing in class, all of us are located in various systems of oppression, either as a member of the dominant group or the targeted group (see p. 91 for discussion of—ism family). All of us have many different identities that add up and intersect to make us who we are. All of us have some **privilege** that advantages us in certain situations, and some **oppression** that we struggle with over the course of our lives. Those of us with privilege can use that privilege to be an **ally** and to work to dismantle systems of oppression for others.

This Wildcat Voices assignment is designed to get you to share one story that highlights how privilege and oppression have functioned in your life. These stories are modeled after the StoryCorps stories we've been listening to recently. When writing this essay/script, think of a story that you want to tell about yourself and your life. Each essay should begin by introducing yourself and the aspect of your identity that your story will highlight. For example,

- "My name is Susan and I am a first-generation college student."

Beyond this common intro, there are many different ways to tell your story. Here are some prompts to choose from to help you think about what you want to say.

- Describe a time when you faced a challenge because of some aspect of your identity. Explain how you overcame that challenge, if you did. Or explain how that challenge continues to shape your experience.
- Describe a time when you acted as an ally for someone else, using your privilege to advocate for others. What was the impact of your intervention?
- Describe a time when someone acted as an ally for you, using their privilege to advocate for you in ways that helped you get to where you are today. What would you want to say to that person if they were in front of you now?

---

[7]This assignment focuses on students' ability to apply course concepts to their own lives, and to use course concepts as a lens through which to narrate and interpret their own experiences. It asks students to reflect on their social location and their embeddedness in systems of Privilege and Oppression. As mentioned in the prompt above, students are asked to complete this assignment after listening to and discussing a variety of clips from StoryCorps, a project whose website describes it as "an American non-profit organization whose mission is to record, preserve, and share the stories of Americans from all backgrounds and beliefs."

5.7   Sample Discussion Prompts

Students will have small group discussions most weeks throughout the semester. These discussion boards will be active on Mondays–Wednesdays. Students will be in the same group through the first unit of the course, unless circumstances warrant moving student(s) to a different group (adds/drops, etc.). Students will be in a different group for the second unit, and also the third, so that they have a chance to talk to different students throughout the semester. The small group discussions will not be graded each week, but instead they will be assessed holistically at the end of each unit. Please look through the assignment rubric to see how to meet expectations in these discussions. Remember that these discussions are worth 20% of your total grade for the course, so they require a significant investment of your time and effort.

For our first small group discussions this week, we will be discussing the assigned reading from the textbook.

As explained in the discussion rubric, each student is required to post **one individual post (between 200 and 350 words)** and a minimum of **two substantive responses to other students' posts (a substantive response is more than just "I agree.")** Each week I will give you some analysis questions to kick off your small group discussions; these discussion questions will pair with the narrated Powerpoint that will be posted at the beginning of each week (for most weeks). For your individual posts, **I don't necessarily expect you to thoroughly answer each and every analysis question that I pose here.** Instead, think of these questions as jumping-off points. For instance, if one of your small group members has answered one question, perhaps you could focus on a different one or two, just to keep the thread interesting.

Critical and thoughtful engagement with each other is encouraged; however, it is important to be respectful in your interactions with other students. Sometimes the tone is hard to read in written form (especially sarcasm or humor), so be sure to do your best to model kindness and generosity when engaging with others.

5.7.1   Week 1 Analysis Questions to Prompt Discussion

1. The textbook reading this week discusses stereotypes of feminists/feminism. Did you hear some of the stereotypes of feminists listed on pp. 5–7? Which ones? Have you heard any others that don't appear in the textbook? What did you make of the textbook discussion of the purposes or functions of these stereotypes?

2. The textbook (p. 10) discusses some Pew research data about young people's beliefs about gender equality and relationships. What were your thoughts about this research? Did it surprise you or did it seem to match up to your friend's and family's beliefs? The textbook then discusses an argument by Stephanie Coontz about the difficulty of putting beliefs about gender equality into practice. What did you think of Coontz's (and the textbook's) analysis of this?

3. The end of the chapter encourages students to practice analysis with three "tests" that help to prompt attention to questions of representation, inclusion, and diversity in popular culture. Think of the last two movies you've watched. Choose one or more of the "tests" discussed at the end of the chapter and determine whether the movies pass it. What's the purpose of doing this sort of critical analysis?

5.7.2 Week 2 Analysis Questions to Prompt Discussion

1. The article we read for small group discussions this week encouraged us to ponder how we might be treated differently if we were a different gender. **Can you give an example of an experience that you had that you think was shaped by your gender?**

2. In particular, this article interviews several transgender men about their experiences before and after their transitions. We haven't yet discussed much about transgender people and identities in this class (but we will!), so this week we can start out with really general questions. **What connections or insights did you have when reading about the experiences of these transgender men? Did you have questions left unanswered?**

3. As I discussed in the narrated PowerPoint for this week, one goal for our small group discussion this week is to try to cultivate empathy across the gender divide—like when Byron Hurt had his "aha" moment in the violence prevention workshop. That means that I am encouraging students to ask themselves questions like: "What can be hard about being a man? (and how is this answer shaped by other aspects of identity, i.e. race, class, sexuality, ability, etc.) What can be hard about being a woman? (and how is this answer shaped by other aspects of identity, i.e. race, class, sexuality, ability, etc.) What can be hard about being non-binary and maybe not feeling like you fit into to either category of 'man' or 'woman'?" **After reading other students' stories, or reflecting on the readings we've done so far, did you have any 'aha' or 'click' moments that you can share?**

5.7.3   Week 3 Analysis Questions to Prompt Discussion

1. This week's materials allow us to learn more about people who are intersex. What were some of your reactions and insights to watching the documentary, *Intersexion*? What questions still remained in your mind after hearing their stories? Where else, if anywhere, have you heard or read about people who are intersex?

2. This week we also were assigned a short blog post that argued the biological sex binary (male or female) is socially constructed to some degree. What were some of the thoughts, reactions, or insights you had when reading this article? Looking at the "Dig Deeper" questions at the end of this post, how would you answer one or more of these questions: Often when people learn that science cannot definitively identify males from females, they dismiss the fact as ridiculous. Why do you think this is? Why aren't male athletes also forced to undergo sex verification? What is the underlying assumption here about the differences between male and female bodies? Explain your answer.

3. Women outperform men in long-distance swimming. For instance, women hold the United States records for 15, 20, 25, 30, and 35 km swims. How does this challenge the logic that supports sex testing only female athletes? Explain your answer. Outside of sports, how does the male/female sex dichotomy limit or oppress people? Explain your answers.

5.7.4   Week 4 Analysis Questions to Prompt Discussion

1. This section of the textbook that we were assigned discussed the concept of gender ranking and gave several examples of how gender ranking plays out in contemporary culture. One of the discussions of gender ranking was about naming practices. What were some of your thoughts and reactions to the discussion of naming practices as a site of gender ranking? What does your name say about gender as a social system? If you'd like, put your first name into the Baby Name Wizard: https://www.babynamew izard.com/ (Links to an external site.) to find out how popular it is by gender. Did you have any questions about this part of the reading?

2. Another example of gender ranking discussed in the textbook reading was about certain career fields and what happens when career fields (like veterinary medicine) become feminized. What were some of your thoughts and reactions to the discussion of career fields as a site of gender ranking? Did you have any questions about this part of the reading?

3. The textbook reading also talked about androcentrism, which is when men (and a certain limited conception of a real "man") is seen as the default, desired, or expected norm. For instance, according to one recent survey, in children's literature male protagonists still outnumber female protagonists by a ratio of 2 to 1. Can you think of other examples of androcentrism in our current cultural landscape? To what extent do you think these things are starting to change? Can you give an example?

5.7.5   Week 5 Analysis Questions to Prompt Discussion

1. This week we read an article by Peggy Orenstein, which was an excerpt from her newish book, *Boys & Sex*. After reading the Orenstein article, what were some of your thoughts, insights, and reactions? Orenstein was trying to illustrate how Man Box culture can sometimes make it hard for men & boys to be allies in the struggle against sexism, to stand up to other men and boys, and to be their authentic selves. Have you seen examples of this in your own life? Have there been times when you have reinforced man box culture? Examples?

2. This week we also read the recently released APA Guidelines for Practice with Men & Boys. What does research show are the negative effects of hypermasculinity or overly restrictive unhealthy masculinity (what is commonly called "toxic masculinity") on men and boys? What difference does race, class, and sexuality make? Why did this announcement receive such backlash from some folks? Are the authors arguing that being a man is bad or that masculinity is always harmful?

5.7.6   Discussion Board Prompt on Family in the Context of the Threshold Concepts of Privilege and Oppression

For this week's discussion post, I would like for you to write a post on this Discussion Board. You will be able to read and "like" other students' posts after you submit your post. This week you will get to choose ONE of the following two prompts:

1. Have a conversation with someone you know who has a child or children under eight years of age. This could be a sibling, cousin, friend, neighbor, co-worker, etc. Ask them how they navigated decisions around work and family when their kid(s) were little (under five years of age): opting-out

of work (for how long?) returning to work soon after birth (how soon?) working extra hours so another parent could stay home? using paid or unpaid family leave? childcare choices? costs of childcare? how did costs of childcare compare to total household earnings? breastfeeding (yes?, no?, how long?, why?—tread lightly here—this can be a very personal and a sensitive topic) career choice (did they choose a career/job intentionally because they thought it was "family-friendly"? did they start a new career/job after returning to the workforce after a hiatus? how did that work out for them?) And any other questions you feel might be relevant. Then, follow the directions below.

OR (if you don't want to talk with someone, or find that too difficult a task)

2. Find a news story that profiles a parent or parents who are navigating decisions about work and family with young kids (under five years of age). It can be a story about how paid family leave is working at the state- or corporate-level, like this: https://www.npr.org/sections/health-shots/2016/10/07/496936072/how-californias-paid-family-leave-law-buys-time-for-new-parents (Links to an external site.) or even a story about what these decisions look like in other countries, like this: https://www.theatlantic.com/family/archive/2020/01/japan-paternity-leave-koizumi/605344/ (Links to an external site).

5.7.7 Discussion Board Prompts on the Threshold Concept of Intersectionality

Group 1: The Opening Illustration for our chapter on intersectionality used breastfeeding as an example. According to the textbook, why is it important to analyze breastfeeding with an intersectional lens? Did this section deepen your understanding of the issue of breastfeeding (especially since we were talking about it recently in class)? If so, how? Any other questions or insights about the opening illustration?
Group 2: This chapter gives a brief overview of the important insights of women of color, working-class women, and lesbian women (among others) that were instrumental in building a more expansive and inclusive movement to end sexism. What were some of your insights and reactions to the examples mentioned? Did some examples resonate with you more than others? Would you add some more recent examples of important critiques to make the movement to end sexism more intersectional?

Group 3: On the bottom of page 151, the textbook tries to illustrate how systems of inequality can be (and most often are) connected. The example the textbook goes on to discuss is how "disability is (or can be) both a cause and a consequence of poverty." Explain and expand on what this means. Are there details that you can add to this point drawn from your own observations and insights?

Group 4: The textbook chapter discusses why it is important to think intersectionally with our approaches to supporting survivors of intimate partner violence. What insights and reactions did you have to the points made about this topic? Had you considered these aspects of the issue before? Are there other points that you would add to help think even more intersectionally?

Group 5: The textbook chapter discusses how masculinity can be classed and racialized by talking about male heads of state and their gender expression and public image. Can you think of another example (not about politicians) of masculinity being shaped by class or race or sexuality in a way that also demonstrates why it is important to think intersectionally? What might we be missing or flattening by talking about the norms of masculinity or the "man box" as if it were the same for all men?

5.7.8 Discussion Board Prompt on Intersectionality That Encourages Metacognition

This week we are continuing our discussion of intersectionality—what it is (and what it's not), why it matters, and how to use an intersectional lens to analyze issues. Our discussion board this week will mostly then be about giving you space to reflect and solidify your understanding of intersectionality as we get closer to the end of the semester and the third skills assessment.

For your discussion post, pick one of the topics mentioned either in the assigned textbook reading on intersectionality or in my narrated slides. Then, write 2–3 paragraphs discussing this topic and reflecting on your understanding of intersectionality thus far. What insights have you had? What is still fuzzy or confusing to you?

5.8 Final Online Discussion: Reflection and Metacognition

In this discussion, your goal will be to reflect on and unpack the learning you have done in this course. You should consider the four threshold concepts that are central to women's and gender studies as a field and discuss how these "lenses" have helped to make the invisible visible and to see differently.

In your first post to the discussion board, describe your growth as a scholar of women's and gender studies; what do you know now, and what do you know how to do now, that you didn't at the beginning of the semester? You might also consider which readings, class activities, or independent analysis strategies were most helpful in developing your grasp of the concept, as well as any course material, teaching and learning activities, or independent experiences that challenged or complicated your understanding (or created barriers for your learning). Ultimately, you want to show how you have arrived at your current level of thinking about the course content and how it has progressed.

In your second post, read over all the contributions by your classmates. Instead of responding to a specific classmates' post, open your own first post, and click on "edit." Add another paragraph to your original post labeled "Updated Thoughts." In a well-developed paragraph, identify at least **two themes** that you see in your classmates' responses. In other words, explain what you see as common experiences, insights, or challenges that your classmates' reflective posts illustrate.

5.9 Accelerated Online Course

5.9.1 Small Group Discussions[8]

You have been assigned a new small-group discussion for this unit. The goal for this Unit discussion is to deepen your understanding of the threshold concepts in GWS studies, particularly how privilege and oppression are structural and systemic. By Tuesday, June 16, complete the reading or listening of

---

[8]Weekly small group discussions are important for practicing new language and for seeing the divergent entry points that classmates bring. It can offer an opportunity for surfacing misconceptions as well as to practice the process skills of perspective-taking and negotiating multiple points of view. Analysis skills are also embedded into the learning task because students are asked to apply concepts from readings to new texts or examples. This assignment worked well to get students talking to each other but requires some set up because of prior expectations students might have for online courses where discussion is not very interactive.

the selected articles from the Unit 2 reading list. Compose a post of about 300 words in which you do the following:

(a) Offer a summary of the key ideas, information, arguments, or data from the two texts you read (include a link to the article(s))
(b) Explain how you see the concepts of Privilege and Oppression (or you could also select another one of our bolded terms from the chapter for a more focused analysis) are illustrated by those texts.

Between Tuesday and Friday, respond to each other's analysis. There is no specified number of posts or responses here but rather an encouragement to read, respond, and converse about the selected readings and how you see this threshold concept as illustrated in these specific texts. The discussion rubric (how I assess your contributions) should be visible to you in the navigation menu. I've also included a link to a jpg. Complete your discussion by **Friday, June 19 and reference in your Unit Reflection Paper**.

5.9.2   Unit Reflection Papers[9]

Learning Objective: We are working throughout this course on achieving several learning outcomes. The reflection papers are one way that you will be able to show what you see are important topics, information, and perspectives reflected in our readings and discussions. In this document that you'll complete for each unit, aim to synthesize (bring together, or integrate) the readings, discussions, and assessments that we've engaged in during the unit. For example, you should probably reference the reading assignments as well as insights you gained from participating the small group conversations with classmates. You might cite or quote from both of those sources, as part of showing your thinking and analysis as you engage with the course material. Here are some more specific goals:

- integrate your current thinking with new information and "lenses" or concepts
- show how your thinking is evolving based on readings and discussion
- ask questions that puzzle, intrigue, or trouble you

---

[9]Unit reflection papers are an opportunity for students to cultivate metacognition (by asking questions, surfacing issues that emerge in discussion, and posing questions about the topics of discussion). Likewise, it is an opportunity to practice analysis skills, and to reflect on the process work of class discussions. Some students are not used to this genre of writing (one that is reflective and integrative) and may require explicit instruction or permission to write informally.

- make connections to previous learning you have done or experiences you have had

Purpose and Goals for You as a Writer

- Show your knowledge (link to or reference information and texts that are influencing your understanding)
- "write to learn"—this is a term from the field of writing studies that means that the cognitive processes of articulating our thinking actually help us concretize our learning. Writing down your thinking helps you figure out what you think!
- Practice academic writing
- Develop the ability to synthesize and analyze complex texts and perspectives
- Hone your own thinking, beliefs, and values around gender, equity, and social structures.

Requirements

- submit your reflection paper by uploading a Word document to the submission box, or copying in a link to a google document
- Aim for about 500–750 words (around 2 pages)
- If you use sources from outside of class, please cite in a recognized documentation style (MLA, APA, etc.), and/or put a link to the source in your document.

5.10 End of Term Assessment: Feminist Praxis Activity and Report[10]

Our class is pretty accelerated and ordinarily I would ask students to do a more expansive feminist praxis project; however, one of the advantages of the short length of time is that feminist praxis can happen everywhere and anywhere, and doesn't necessarily require a lot of planning or work—it can be changed to how we live and what we do every day. So in that vein, I'm asking you to wrap up the course by engaging in an **Act of Feminist Praxis and Report**, which will require this:

---

[10]the Feminist Praxis activity and report are ways for students to build on the process and analysis skills they have learned and the Content knowledge they have gained. Praxis requires applying and integrating new knowledge into a context outside of the classroom.

1. Review the resources below, or feel free to do other social media investigation or web searching to identify an issue that is important to you and that you are interested in taking a small step or activity toward feminist praxis, as it fits the definition outlined in our textbook: "strategies that feminist activists and educators use to effect change that supports gender justice" (193)
2. For our Unit 4 discussion component, you'll create a short proposal or plan that you'll share on our class google doc.
3. Because of our super-accelerated timeline, these praxis activities can be pretty modest. Maybe it's to write a letter or create a social media post, or some act of change that you want to engage within your local social circle, workplace, or town. As long as you can explain how it fulfills the definition of Feminist Praxis (or antiracist, anti-ableist, etc.), and of course should be some type of activity that is meaningful or important to you.

Requirements

- Participate in the posting and giving feedback on your Act of Feminist Praxis: Post your idea, a description, and rationale. Reply to 2 classmates' ideas with comment on the right-hand column—things they might consider, outlets for their activity—anything that will help them fulfill their activity goals.
- Engage in your praxis activity! This can take place in the last week of class.
- Submit a final Feminist Praxis Report. It should be about **750 words and do the** following:

  - Describe your Act of Feminist Praxis—what did you do, why did you do it
  - What were the results or outcomes, if any; *provide explicit documentation of your activity*. Types of documentation might include the following:
    - Screenshots of a social media effort
    - Copies of an email sent and/or received in response
    - Video or audio files that illustrate your activity
    - Some other documentation that helps make your activity and results visible to others
  - Explain how you see the activity as connected to and reflective of the course content. Make explicit connections to readings that have been assigned or that you have selected as part of our discussions.
  - Add any reflections you have about the activity.

Ideas for Feminist Praxis: This is not an exhaustive list but is a place to start as you think about a way you might want to engage in an act of praxis, bystander intervention or upstander intervention for your Feminist Praxis report assignment.

- 75 Things White People Can Do for Racial Justice
- Dear White People, This is What We Want You to Do
- Scaffolded Anti-Racist Resources
- 35 Practical Steps Men Can Take To Support Feminism
- Resources for Accountability and Actions for Black Lives
- The History of Racism in America | History
- Opinion | America, This Is Your Chance
- The History of Racism in America | History
- Narrowing Wikipedia's gender gap with NWSA – Wiki Education
- Five ways the NWSA-Wiki Ed partnership has made an impact
- BEST PRACTICES FOR SERVING LGBTQ STUDENTS
- Ableism 101 Workshop Series: (Brief) History of Disability Activism & Disability Rights | Disability Resources
- UNDERSTANDING AND CHALLENGING ABLEISM.

5.11   Sample Rubrics for Assessing Course Activities[11]

See Tables 5.1, 5.2, and 5.3.

---

[11]Though not every instructor embraces the use of rubrics for assessment, we include several here to show how student learning and achievement of outcomes can be described at multiple levels. Criteria are also explicitly named so that both students and teachers have an understanding of what is valued by the assignment.

Table 5.1 Skills Assessments

	Student work achieving the learning goal at an Advanced level will…	Student work achieving the learning goal at an Proficient level will…	Student work achieving the learning goal at an Competent level will…	Student work achieving the learning goal at an Developing level will…
Framing and analysis	Accurately use the threshold concept(s) to frame the analysis, identifying overlaps and relationships between them Accurately and insightfully use the threshold concept to demonstrate a feminist stance	Accurately use the threshold concept to frame the analysis Accurately use the threshold concept(s) to demonstrate a feminist stance	Use the threshold concept(s) to frame the analysis, perhaps with some limitations or misunderstandings Use the threshold concept as a lens to demonstrate a feminist stance	Not use the threshold concept(s) to frame the analysis Not use the threshold concept as a lens to demonstrate a feminist stance
Evidence	Provide multiple pieces of evidence from the course material and additional, non-course-based examples to illustrate the threshold concept(s)	Provide one or more pieces evidence from the course material to illustrate the threshold concept(s)	Provide at least one piece of evidence from course material to illustrate the threshold concept(s)	Not provide evidence and examples from the course material or other sources to illustrate the threshold concept
Accuracy	Accurately understand the threshold concepts(s) and identify both course-based and new, independently generated evidence that illustrates it	Accurately understand the threshold concepts(s) and identify course-based evidence that illustrates it	Demonstrate an accurate understanding of the threshold concept (s)	Misunderstand or mischaracterize the threshold concept(s)

Table 5.2 Unit Reflection Papers

	Advanced	Proficient	Competent	Developing
Comprehension of Texts	demonstrates completion of an accurate, insightful comprehension of readings	demonstrates completion and accurate comprehension of readings	demonstrates completion and comprehension of readings	does not demonstrate completion or comprehension of readings
Inquiry, Analysis, Reflection	effectively and insightfully reflects on the content and skills introduced in the unit	effectively reflects on the content and skills introduced in the unit	effectively reflects on content and skills introduced in the unit, perhaps with additional room for development	does not effectively or accurately reflect on content and skills introduced in the unit
Requirements	meaning is clear; meets assignment guidelines and constraints (reflection, analysis); sufficiently explains and supports thinking	meaning is clear; meets assignment guidelines and constraints (reflection, analysis); sufficiently explains and supports thinking	meaning is clear; meets assignment guidelines and constraints (reflection, analysis); sufficiently explains and supports thinking	meaning is unclear; does not meet assignment guidelines and constraints (reflection, analysis); does not sufficiently explain thinking

Table 5.3 Unit Discussion Rubric

	Advanced	Proficient	Competent	Developing
Engagement with Classmates	Posts and responses use multiple pieces of evidence from the text(s) and discussions to insightfully and accurately summarize and synthesize peers' viewpoints	Posts and responses use evidence from the text(s) and discussions to accurately summarize and synthesize peers' viewpoints	Posts and responses summarize and synthesize peers' viewpoints in a general way	Posts and responses minimally synthesize or summarize and are supported by opinion and/or summary. Posts do not demonstrate the writer has read and understood classmate ideas
Comprehension of Texts	Posts and responses accurately and specifically discuss the relevant text(s) in detail	Posts and responses accurately and specifically discuss the relevant text(s)	Posts and responses discuss the relevant text(s) in general	Posts and responses discuss the text(s) minimally
Synthesis and Analysis	Posts and responses demonstrate analysis of readings, understanding of and engagement with new ideas, and contribute more than summary to the discussions. Post and response draws from the readings and course material in explicit ways	Posts and responses show analysis of readings, integration with previous knowledge, and contribute more than summary to the discussions. Post and response draws from the readings and course material	Posts and responses show developing analysis, use sufficient textual evidence to demonstrate understanding of readings. Post and response draws from the readings and course material in explicit ways	Posts and responses use insufficient evidence to support analysis; posts and responses are mostly summary

(continued)

Table 5.3 (continued)

	Advanced	Proficient	Competent	Developing
Requirements	Posts and responses exceed all assignment expectations, and meet conventions, and deadlines	Posts and responses meet assignment expectations, conventions, and deadlines	Posts and responses meet most assignment expectations, conventions, and deadlines	Posts and responses meet a few assignment expectations, conventions, and deadlines

Index

© The Editor(s) (if applicable) and The Author(s) 2021
H. Hassel et al., *A Guide to Teaching Introductory Women's and Gender Studies*,
https://doi.org/10.1007/978-3-030-71785-8

The manufacturer's authorised representative in the EU is Springer
Nature Customer Service Centre GmbH, Europaplatz 3, 69115 Heidelberg,
Germany. If you have any concerns regarding our products, please
contact ProductSafety@springernature.com

Printed and bound by CPI Group (UK) Ltd, Croydon, CR0 4YY
29/04/2026
02099459-0015